The Hog
the Dog
&
Iron Horse
the

By the same author

Bass of Shades

The Complete Cornish Live Gig Review

9 Years 84000 Words

Road Dog Publications was formed in 2010 as an imprint dedicated to publishing the best in books on motorcycling and adventure travel. Visit us at www.roaddogpub.com.

The Hog the Dog & the Iron Horse; Travels through America
Copyright © 2018 Alex Kendall
All rights reserved.

ISBN 978-1-890623-87-6
Library of Congress Control Number: 2022950860

An Imprint of Lost Classics Book Company
This book also available in eBook format at online booksellers. ISBN 978-1-890623-88-3

THE HOG
THE DOG
& THE
IRON HORSE

TRAVELS THROUGH AMERICA

BY

Alex Kendall

Publisher
Lake Wales, Florida

This book is dedicated, as always, to my better halves

Julie, Sam and Jess.

And to Janet Deaville and Teej.

About the Author

Alex Kendall is a Cornishman at the tail end of his stupid life. He has worked (against his wishes) in engineering for most of his days, due to geography and a lazy gene that he has yet to bother looking for.

His father had travelled the world three times before Alex was even born, and so his family home was full of artifacts like African masks, tribal drums made out of animal skins with horns shoved in them, French duelling swords, stuffed baby alligators, etc. It was like a British museum; everywhere you looked, there were things that didn't belong. On one wall was a large print of *Guernica* by Pablo Picasso. It was that sort of house.

His teenage years were spent hitchhiking (due to finances and being ugly enough to not bother the most desperate of child molesters). This led him to many thumb-based adventures, including one to Paris at the end of the '80s to avoid the music of

Simply Red. Sadly, he found the bobble-headed lothario even more popular on the Continent and returned.

There have been breaks in his so-called 'engineering career,' such as when he put himself through university to become a teacher, ending up in The Bahamas. Having watched the locals casually shoot at the police on day one, nearly chop his own fingers off on an ceiling fan on day two, and then be informed by his employers that the island was considered the fourth murder capital in the world on day three, he returned to Cornwall (UK), at the end of the last century, to become the best 'still alive' Dad in the world.

Running parallel to his exotic life, he has been writing constantly. As a child, he drew his own comics, kept a very tedious diary, and wrote and recorded his own terrible songs. As an adult, he learnt his lessons and moved on to run his own fanzine and do some freelance work in the national music press, which found him rubbing shoulders with artists of a much higher calibre than Mick Hucknell (thankfully). This then led him to writing books, when an unexpected biography piece uncovered too many fascinating details for the planned article.

His first travel book, *The Hog, The Dog, & The Iron Horse*, came about after a life long love of the beat writers' work and a desire to see beyond the façade the media bombards us with. He traveled through America using the iconic Greyhound bus, the Amtrak train, and an Indian motorcycle. He wanted to see the 'real' America and experience life on the road once again.

Along the way he travelled 20,000 miles, destroyed his spinal column, got mistaken for a model, had breakfast with a stuntman, survived for three days on two packets of nuts, hung out with gold miners, ex-cons, and famous comedians, nearly drowned on a motorcycle, and became a drug smuggler. The book is a combined guide book, travel journal, and a warning to dreamers. It is also very funny and very rude.

He owns far too many books already, but it didn't stop him getting hold of a copy of Zoe Cano's first brilliant adventure, *Bonneville Go Or Bust*, and it probably won't stop him buying more.

CONTENTS

About the Author v

The Dog 1

Stage One—Planning 5

Stage Two–Riding the Dog 17
Still Cornwall.. 21
Cornwall...23
Cornwall ... to Heathrow...25
Heathrow to New York City 27
New York City..39
New York City 47
New York, Richmond, Winston-Salem, Knoxville...... 55
Menphis, Little Rock, Amarillo 61
Pheonix, Los Angeles 67
Los Angeles ... .83
Los Angeles ... Still... 87

Los Angeles 91
Los Angeles . . . Bye Bye LA LA................................ 93
Stage Three-The Iron Horse 95
Los Angeles, Flagstaff, Finding Johnny McDonald 97
Albuquerque, Kansas City....................................... 105
Kansas City, Chicago 111
Chicago, New York City.. 117
New York City, Deathrow.. 127
Heathrow... 135
What Happened Next 139

Stage Four, The Return, The Hog.............................. 143
New York City... 145
New York City... 153
New York City, Chicago 157
Chicago, Tipton... 165
Tipton... 171
Tipton, Hannibal 175
Hannibal, Memphis 183
Memphis.. 189
Memphis.. 199
Menphis... 199
Memphis, Texarkana 207
Texarkana, Dallas... 209

Stage Five, Postscript 217

Acknowledgements 219

THE DOG

Most travel books start with an exciting and somewhat bizarre event and then go on to tell you how the author ended up in such a sticky pickle. As anyone who knows me would expect, this one doesn't. It starts with a damning review of an American rock band.

Wednesday 11th April 2012

Apparently ' . . . the journey of a thousand miles starts with a single step.'

And ' . . . the journey is better than the destination.'

But the Journey, of mid-Atlantic rock fame, were crap.

(No, seriously, they were utter bog water.)

The seventies and eighties were full of middle of the road,

mild mannered morons, macerating music for the masses (as Sally Freedman, top rock journalist of Bad News fame, might say). The only connection to a journey that they had was the distance you'd be prepared to travel to avoid having to listen to them. I mean, 'Don't Stop Believin',' really? Some of us never started, pal. How did they ever sustain a forty year career with such an abysmal collection of tunes?

At this point you may be wondering why I've started a travel book with such a damning review of 'one of America's top AOR bands,' well if not now, then when? But to be honest, there is a connection. And here it is—*middle of the road* is a phrase that I hate. It is the lowest common denominator in all situations. Sitting on the fence, non-committal, no opinions or too scared to voice them, the easy option, the colour beige, etc.—all mediocrity and no ambition. Life is full of this attitude; nobody wants to rock the boat; everyone's got their heads down. Well I'm not having it! Life is so fucking short, and as you get older you begin to realise how much of it has been wasted.

A few years ago, I took the family on a holiday that involved an old gypsy caravan of dubious standing being tugged around the back roads of Ireland by a belligerent old cob horse called Matty. Yes, we called that a holiday. We had an eighteen month old baby, and everyone said we were crazy. They thought we should all go to a hotel somewhere hot like Spain and enjoy all the sweaty British tourists with their inflatables on the Costa Del Bollocks. Well, it turned out fine; we had a whale of a time and now have some great stories to tell about German firemen and the persistence of Irish rain. Nobody actually died. I mean, there was that choking incident, but no fatalities.

So 'fall into line'? Fuck that for a game of soldiers. Let me make some memories worth having, because in the end, that's all we leave behind. As The King Blues said, 'Participate, don't spectate— become the view . . . '

Journey (the band) is the epitome of the bland, easy option life that everyone seems to gravitate towards and thus, they, and their fans, are my enemy. And yet their name implies some sort of adventure, an unusual experience, maybe even . . . a little danger? Well in fact, it's just false bloody advertising. A bunch of fat sweaty blokes with facial hair looking like they'd pop a frock on at the drop of a hanky is not my idea of a journey, thank you very much. What I want is some Kerouac, Kesey, or Hunter S. Basically, I want the truth. I want to know what America is like when the cameras aren't pointing at it.

So this is how it happened:

Some bastard invented the National Lottery. Then they foisted it upon the British public, most of whom had no interest in gambling until it became as easy as buying their daily paper, and then the idea of becoming a millionaire without earning the money was soon acceptable. After a short time, a European Lottery also reared its head, with even more stupidly high figures for winnings. Once the bench mark was set, the idea of what you would do with your winnings became a common conversation (as if you'd ever really win. I mean, some of the conversations were with people who never even bought a bloody ticket in the first place). But eventually, we had to consider the issue like everyone else. Somewhere way back in my memory, I must have seen *Easy Rider* (the cult biker '60s movie starring Peter Fonda and Dennis Hopper), and it must have left an impression, because I decided I'd like to spend six months travelling across the States on a Harley chop with my best friend, really 'living' and seeing what freedom meant. I suppose I could've just looked in a dictionary, but I'm an awkward sod.

Well so much for that, and if you haven't seen the film yet, I won't spoil the ending for you here (they all die) (I lied, ha!). And the years went by. Then, out of the blue, I won a weekend in New York City for two people in a swanky, top class hotel, and so I took my wife with me. It happened to be her fortieth birthday, and I had already taken her on holidays to London and Paris earlier in the year, so this was the icing on both our cakes, (although I prefer fresh cream myself) (. . . ooer, madam).

Suddenly, I had a chance to witness America first hand, and although a short visit to arguably the least American location in America (NYC is truly a world of its own), the city didn't let me down at all. In fact, it gave me a taste for more. I got back to Cornwall afterwards and realised that a version of my lottery dream was possible if I did it right away. So I put it to Julie (my wife) and she was totally supportive (as I'd hoped she would be). I had spent many of our early years together watching her go abroad with her family and friends while I stayed at home and had never complained, so I suppose this was my reward in some ways. Of course, we had children now to consider, and finances were getting tighter as the days drew by. But Julie stuck by me. I think she could see it in my eyes that I needed this thing.

I'd hitch-hiked over to France in my early years, before Julie, and had travelled rough for many years even before then, so I wasn't as daunted as some might be.

I had to adapt some of my lottery dream details though—there wasn't enough money or time to learn how to ride a motorcycle (or 'hog' as some call them), and so I decided to use the other land travel available, hire car. Looked into that, and it was far too expensive. So next up was the world famous icon that is the Greyhound coach (or 'riding the dog,' as it was referred to in the States). That was stupidly cheap from NYC to LA (about £80), and the Amtrak train back (what the native Americans used to call the 'iron horse') from LA to NYC was only about £120. Again, silly money, considering the distance, time zones covered, and compared to our own country, it was a ridiculous bargain. Christ, the journey crosses four time zones in the USA. It costs me £30 just to get 300 miles to London by our own coach company (the less iconic National Depress).

So the stage was set; I was going to travel across a massive country I'd never really been to, completely on my own. A daunting combined journey (including flights) of roughly twelve thousand miles.

I thought, 'That's like a thousand journeys to work (for me).'

And then I thought, 'but without the work part of that equation. That's a thousand days off work for me.'

Suddenly, it seemed like a better prospect.

Stage One-Planning
(I'm a Virgo—it's a disease, don't even go there)

The big things—1) The Visa. This is America, and regardless of what that buffoon Trump says, they don't just let anyone in; you still have to have the right paperwork. Now, in this case it's called an ESTA ('Electronic System for Travel Authorization'—acronym fans); it costs fourteen dollars online and lasts for two years. You don't need to print it out or anything; the customs never ask you about it. Their computer checks up on you, and unless you're an utter bastard, you should get a confirmation fairly quickly (like in twenty-four hours). Admittedly, it's a bit of a tense twenty-four hours as you wonder what they might uncover about your murky past. Is scrumping apples considered a retrospective crime in the twenty-first century? What about that time . . . ? (I'll let you fill in your own personal embarrassments here.) Well, once you pay your fee, it can seem like a bloody long time until you get the confirmation.

Okay, so assuming you've got the all clear, the ESTA's in the bag, and now you need to move on to the next priority.

2) Money and Timetable—It seems obvious, but have you got enough to pay for your journey? The Internet quickly becomes your best friend (if it isn't already), as hours of your life get soaked up cross checking prices of flights and dates. Soon enough, the word, *availability* will become your catch phrase as your try to juggle what's on offer with what you can actually use.

I had a maximum of seventeen days that I could use, and so, because of the unknown mystical forces that control flight timetables, I had to find the cheapest flights to and from New York. The perfect times would be compromised, because if I travelled at a slightly less convenient time, I could save £110 or something. It made no sense. Sometimes it works to travel by two different companies so that their timetables suit you better. (It's what travel agents do to get paid. It's like the self-service tills at supermarkets, but this time you actually 'save' money, not time.) Unfortunately, at the same time as you are looking at the flight times, you also need to look at the other travel parts of the journey. It's all very well getting a cheap flight, but if it doesn't match up with the Amtrak or Greyhound timetables, you'll be left at the roadside; time to learn how to juggle.

So I started with the days I was going to take off work, my seventeen days of freedom. They were fixed by the Queen. Yeah, that's what I said, the bloody Queen of England made this all possible. Liz was celebrating fifty years on the throne or something and gave her subjects an extra day off work; a public holiday for the whole country to party. I chose to use mine by leaving the country. Within my seventeen days there were two bank holidays, and so my timetable was pretty much fixed, so what could I get to fit within my personal boundaries?

After getting a rough idea what the flight would cost (not fixing dates, just a ballpark figure), I turned my attention to the Greyhound and Amtrak timetables and costs. Well the costs were a joke, so I looked at the dates and time each took to cross the country. The Greyhound was about three and a half days from NYC to LA, and the Amtrak strangely seemed to be about the same. So I counted out eight days to those bits of the journey and obviously had nine days in hand. A couple of days in NYC at the start and end of the round journey took up another four, and that left me with five in LA; sorted.

The parameters were coming together. At the British end of the journey we had a night bus to Heathrow and an afternoon trip back at the end (about £30-ish). The flights, because of the time zones they crossed, sort of cancelled each other out a bit. One was nine hours and the other was seven, so somewhere up in the air we travelled through time. Anyway, you know how it works. (Although I still have trouble actually with the theory of 'aviation' but content myself with the belief that, like comedy and frogs, if I don't dissect it too much, it'll just continue to 'work'.)

So now I had a rough plan of action, the fun really started:

3) The Details—I tend to read magazines backwards; I don't know why, but I do. I've probably got a syndrome or something. Whatever. Anyway, I find that, like creating art, if you start in the middle and work your way out, things often look better, and when planning, this is the way I do things: I start with the sandwich filler and get that sorted before I commit to the bread. In this case, the heart of the journey was the coach and train, and so those were the first things I paid for after the ESTA. Yeah, that's right; I paid for two massive eight time zone-crossing journeys before I had confirmed that I would even be able to be in the country that they were to take place in. My thinking was that, with a combined cost of £200, they were in fact the least expensive part of the journey, and if it all went tits up, at least I wouldn't lose my shirt (it's funny how phrases can come back to haunt you, isn't it?).

So I had the dates of the coach and train sorted; receipts were printed up. (In fact, if I'm honest, I did print out my ESTA too, because I'm naturally cautious and like to have my arse covered when I've got nobody to fall back upon.) Here's a thing—Greyhound (amongst almost everybody in America I spoke to) don't expect people from abroad to book tickets on their coaches, and online its quite a thing to understand. Firstly, you can't pick up your tickets (or print them out online) from just any old station. I had to make some trans-Atlantic phone calls eventually to finally understand that I had to pick up the tickets from a certain station in NYC (The Port Authority Bus Station), and then things would be fine. You have a confirmation email, and you need your passport to get the Greyhound company self-service machines to print out your collection of tickets (in my case about ten individual tickets). Amtrak just lets you print out a ticket to carry with you that you exchange for an allocated seat in LA. The first hurdle is now jumped.

And now we work our way out from the centre (missing out accommodation for the moment), finally committing to the flights. I had the dates and, with the two days free at either end of the journey, a bit of a buffer zone to find the ideal flights. After trawling the websites of aircraft companies, airports, flight operators, travel agents, and random blogs, I came to 'dialaflight.com,' who seemed to have the best prices on the timetable I was looking at. £566 gave me two flights with Delta Airlines at either end of my journey between Heathrow and JFK. Now, Dial a Flight were the cheapest, and that may not suit everybody, because obviously, to hold that accolade you may need to cut costs, but with my limited experience at this time, it was hard to spot where their savings were made. They were quick to take my money over the phone ('dial' a flight after all). You couldn't book online, although the details were all there to look at; you had to speak to someone to actually pay. This allowed a little sales patter to be involved, and my costs seemed to increase from the original online prices—now, I don't mind that too much, as long as they don't take the piss. The online prices were about £100 cheaper than the £566 I ended up paying. The reason for this was, apparently, that the flight operators were changing the prices all the time due to fuel costs. Flim-flam, as far as I'm concerned, but I paid over the phone and got the email confirmation soon afterwards.

Now here's a thing; I don't know if its specific to Dial a Flight, but between when I paid on the 14th October and when I flew on the 25th May the following year, they emailed me at least seven times telling me that the flights were either amended or, more disturbingly, cancelled. At first, this caused quite a bit of stress, as you can imagine, with the days clicking down and the emails popping into my inbox on a random, but seemingly more regular, basis. After about the sixth or seventh, I became strangely ambivalent. I was in a place where I transcended the logics of reality; not for the last time on this adventure, I was unusually unconcerned with the possibility of failure. It was almost an out of body experience; I seemed to be watching myself, as if in a movie, with little or no control of the outcome and thus no need to worry about it. It's hard to explain, but there was a serenity about me that I'd never felt before.

Now, I'm a bugger for a checklist, so here's one for you:
ESTA—paid & confirmed
Greyhound—booked & paid
Amtrak—booked & paid
Flights—booked & paid

So far so good, now let's have a look at that other cheap bit of the journey; the National Depress coach journeys to and from Heathrow. They had to link up to the flights booked, and so they bloody well did. Well, to be honest, I like to spend time in airports (twenty-seven hours in Miami International in 1999, but that's another story), and this would be no exception. I like to make sure, having spent a lot of money, that I don't miss flights because of some bell-end in Stevenage that can't drive his car causes a traffic jam while the emergency services attempt to mop up his internal organs off the fast lane before teatime. So I give all travel that I can't control myself as large a buffer zone as I can, time-wise. This time, the cross over between bus journey and flight out of Heathrow was about seven hours on the way out and two or three on the way back. It's a long two hundred and fifty mile journey from Cornwall to Heathrow, and anything could hold us up on that seven-hour trip; mechanical breakdown, accident, nuclear strike, pasty boarder control. And you wouldn't want to miss your flight out after all this effort. However, missing the one back is never such a bother for some reason.

Booking the National Express is easy enough online, and they email you a barcoded ticket to wave at the driver when you board, if you print it out. They do restrict you actually buying the ticket until about three months before you travel (which is a bugger when you're planning a road trip eight months in advance), but they rarely don't have a seat available when you look them up. Apparently, you can also now wave your smart phone at the driver, and some sort of receipt will be electronically exchanged. I have no further information or desire to find out about this, so if you're that sort of person, I guess you'll already know and be shouting at me already, telling me to 'get with the times, granddad,' or some such. Regardless, this is how I did it, and it worked fine for me. If by the time you are reading this we have moved to a completely paperless society—I pity you.

Now on to the exciting, and final, booking beforehand part—the accommodation. I had three separate stops to cater for: two in New York and one in Los Angeles. So obviously, we are thinking hotels, motels, B&Bs, etc., but just at this moment in history there was a new thing starting to take off: I'm talking about AIRBNB. Yeah, once upon a time kids, it didn't even exist (and this was even before Uber taxis too, if you can imagine that). In case you are still unaware of the AIRBNB phenomena, it's a way for travellers to rent spaces to stay in stranger's homes for a fraction of a hotel's cost. These 'spaces' can be anything from a bed in a garage, someone's couch, a private bedroom, or even the whole place. The advantages are clear: you save money, you get to meet locals and hang out with non-tourists; it's like a home from home, and it's safe. As a traveller, you get to vet the owners and accommodation before you pay, via other people's reviews, and as an owner, you can vet the traveller and refuse to let them stay if they're not your cup of tea. Travellers get reviewed by the people they've stayed with and have to pay online before they stay, so it's a very safe and secure system. It had started in America and was slowly unfolding across the planet, but at this stage it was still a sort of underground thing. I found out all about it after I had booked and paid for my hotel in New York City (typical).

My choice of hotel in New York was dictated by my initial search online—'cheap accommodation in New York city.' Google did it's stuff, and I was soon looking at what can only be described as my ideal hotel. The Hotel Carter was perfect. I couldn't believe my eyes when I saw the cost and location—$99 a night and three blocks from Times Square, in the heart of the theatre district. (That was £62.76 at the time and bang in the centre of town.) It was an unbelievable bargain, and I snapped it up as quickly as my fingers could move over the keyboard. Two nights on the way in and two nights on the way back were duly booked, and £280 (including taxes and services fees) left my bank account. Then I looked into the history of my new favourite place to stay in New York.

For most of its life, from 1930 to 1976, it had been called Dixie Hotel and went from 1,000 rooms initially, down to 700 after some bugger knocked a wing off the building. It originally had its own bus station incorporated into the twenty-four story accommodation, (I'm assuming on one of the lower levels). Within a couple of years of construction, the original hotel owners went bankrupt, and the hotel and bus station were sold off to pay their debts. Then in 1932, Roy S. Hubbell, the head of the new management team that had just taken over the running of the hotel, died in the building at the age of fifty-five. In 1942 the Dixie was sold to the Carter Hotels Corp., who waited until 1976 to rename the hotel, just before selling it to a Vietnamese businessman called Truong.

Within the building, over the years, there has been the aforementioned bus station, a laundry, a 250 seat theatre, a nightclub, and a restaurant. By the 1980s, nearly two hundred families were living permanently in the hotel, and the city sued the owners for consistent health and safety violations. By 1984, the city was using the hotel to house homeless people but had to stop shortly afterwards due to foul living conditions.

Five people have committed suicide in the hotel over the years, and four others have been murdered in it, including a baby beaten to death in 1983, a women thrown out of a top floor window in 1987, and in 2007 a former member's of the Goth rock band The Nuns body was discovered wrapped in bin liners under the bed in one of the hotel rooms.

It was voted 'the dirtiest hotel in the US in 2009' by *USA Today* and won a similar award from Trip Advisor three years in a row. Bed bugs, other infestations, and safety issues have given Hotel Carter a reputation that I found immensely attractive for some strange reason. The idea that something so bad could exist in a city that claimed to have been 'cleaned up' appealed to my sense of irony, I guess. I'd never have considered staying there with loved ones, but as a solo traveller looking for adventure, it was the ideal first location. Come on, wouldn't you want to stay there? Now keep in mind that my only other experience of hotels in New York was the ridiculous five-star W Hotel on 5th Avenue, so this would certainly give me the other end of the spectrum.

Well, that was New York sorted; two nights on the way in and two nights on the way out. Next up was the accommodation at the other end, in Los Angeles. I thought I'd try AIRBNB, because it had been publicised as cheaper than a hotel, and knowing the cost of New York (generally), I assumed LA would be similar. I never even considered looking at hotel prices, but instead trawled the AIRBNB site for areas that I thought I'd like to stay within the city. I say 'areas,' because it's much bigger than I'd imagined. It's not so much a city, as another country. They say that in a country pushing 300 million, more than twenty-five per cent live in LA—I don't know how true that is, but it took a hell of a long time for me to find the right place to stay. I avoided Compton, for the obvious reasons (I didn't want that much adventure) and tried to find a place within budget near to Laurel Canyon, where my old college buddy, Ian Webber, now lived. There were hostels on the beach for £17 a night, and garage space accommodation for £20, rooms for £40, and everything upwards, but I eventually picked a self-contained room in the Hollywood Hills for £45 a night. The place was at the top of the hill, on the edge of the Mulholland Dam, just past Moby's house on Creston Drive. It claimed a Beatles connection and was just around the corner from the Hollywood Bowl. The owners, Corey and Jackie Adams, were in the music business and seemed very nice, so I sent them my money, and we agreed on the dates that I intended staying with them. After the initial deal was struck, we continued to communicate and got to know each other better, so that by the time I arrived, it was more like staying with friends than strangers. Less than £250 gave me five nights, self-catering in Los Angeles, in 2011, and I considered that a bargain. As I say, there were (and probably still are) cheaper places to stay, but I wanted a bit of comfort waiting for me at the end of three and a half days on a bus. I may have chosen differently if I'd flown into town (as they say).

I checked Trip Advisor, and nobody had died in the building or written a shitty review about it, so it seemed like a good, if not slightly boring choice. However, apart from the obvious luxury that I was planning for myself, I also needed somewhere quiet to write, so this had to be a consideration for my personal choice this time.

So, now we had the accommodation sorted. Let's look at that old list again . . .

ESTA—paid & confirmed
National Depress—booked & paid
Greyhound—booked & paid
Amtrak—booked & paid
Flights—booked & paid
Accommodation—booked & paid.

What are we missing? That's right; insurance. Because we are old, and because we are sensible, and because we are leaving loved ones behind, and because we are fearful for our little lives, we MUST have insurance.

Insurance to claim back if the flight is cancelled. Insurance to claim back if the bus company goes bust after a hundred years of business (started in 1914, history fans). Insurance to claim back if the hotel's bugs stage a coup and take over the running of the business and refuse to honour the previous management's agreements. Insurance to claim back if the train is hijacked by Native Americans on horseback demanding payment for the generations of abuse dealt them by these European religious nutters that invaded their country all those years ago and have since portrayed them at almost every conceivable opportunity to be nothing less than savages. But by far, the most important insurance you need to think about is the one that will pay for any medical bills that you may incur. America is a nightmare when it comes to healthcare. Just the cost of an ambulance to take you to a hospital could set you back $2,000, so you really don't want to consider travelling over there without some form of medical insurance, my friend. I got my travel insurance online with a company called Cheaper Travel Insurance, which gave me medical expenses of up to five million pounds, repatriation costs of up to five million pounds, and a personal liability of up to one million pounds for the princely sum of £13.20 back in 2010. I imagine it may be slightly more expensive now, but not something to be forgotten about. I wouldn't worry too much in Europe, due to our on-going deals within the EU (this will obviously change as the current political situation changes), but anywhere else in the world and I'd say that it's as important as spending money (and what other type of money is there?).

Anyway, here it is on the list now:
ESTA—paid & confirmed
National Compressed (Express)—booked & paid
Greyhound—booked & paid
Amtrak—booked & paid
Flights—booked & paid
Accommodation—booked & paid
Medical Insurance—paid

The list is nearly complete now. (I bet you're almost as excited as I am, aren't you?) At this stage, all the really important things are sorted. Obviously, your passport is in date, and last I heard, the Americans like you to have at least six months left to run on it before you enter their country, which is fair enough, I guess. Now it's the frivolous stuff; your spending money, choosing your suntan factor, and planning when to shout, 'Bomb!' in airports, just for a laugh.

Back in the day, we were told that Travellers Cheques were the safest thing to have, because if they got lost or stolen, the bank would let you have some more to replace them. And I can even remember using some myself as a kid hitching around France and the obvious annoyance the French bank staff showed me as I tried to cash them. But times have changed, Granddad, and now it's all direct debit and digital what-have-yous. So I looked at the options—

Cashpoint cards (both debit and credit)

These seem to be a safe option, but what a surprise—they come with a nasty sting in the tale. Both cards involve charges for using them abroad. Firstly, a per centage of your withdrawal (I think 2.4% was mentioned at the time), and then the buggers have the nerve to charge you again for actually just having used the cash machine and creating 'transaction charges.' So for each withdrawal you could get charged anything around five per cent. A bill that you'd receive when you got home, I hasten to add.

However, the credit card had an instant credit limit of £2,000, which I figured would get me a flight out of anywhere home to the UK in the event of an emergency. I was told that if I didn't use it, there would be no charge, so to me that was a great bit of free insurance that seemed foolish to turn my nose up at. I had never owned a credit card before, though, and thus didn't know you had to 'verify' it before you could use it to draw out any money. This, of course, was something I learnt once back in the UK afterwards and made it completely useless on my forthcoming journey. Ignorance is bliss, though, eh?

Travellers Cheques

Nobody thought I was being serious about these, did they?

Cash

There's a limit of £10K in cash that you can to leave the country with apparently, so that's that one out of the window, eh? But seriously, the one problem with this is the possibility of robbery or loss. When it's gone, it's gone. (Actually you can even get insurance for this eventuality, apparently, but I haven't looked into that.) So obviously, I chose cash.

I worked out that I could save enough money before I went so that I would have around a hundred dollars a day to live off, which I considered OK, as for at least six days I'd be in transit and unable to spend much. So that was $1,500 in cash, please. In the intervening months before I travelled, I saved a bit more, and as the exchange rate was so good at the time (around $1.58 to the pound), I was able to travel with $2,500 cash on me.

I know.

But I had a cunning plan. I didn't look like a tourist, and so thus, I wouldn't look like I had any money anyway. I wore my only pair of jeans, my only T-shirt (an old Ramones one), my battered old bikers jacket, and a pair of ratty old converse sneakers. I carried no luggage at all, just one small canvas shoulder bag that looked like a student might've used for lunch, and I smoked roll ups. I looked like I couldn't afford the Greyhound bus fare, let alone a flight. But this was exactly the way I wanted to be perceived; invisible. I was on a mission to observe the real America, not the media driven bullshit, the over-hyped rubbish that nobody with half a brain cell believed. I wanted to meet the people who, like me, are just going about their business trying to survive.

Of course, I did have a slight problem in that I was a 6'4" tall, white, Englishman with an accent that I assumed would betray me every time I opened my mouth. We shall see.

Don't bother with suntan lotion—this isn't a bloody beach holiday. And don't shout 'Bomb!' in airports. If you must shout something try, 'Bamboleo!' (the Gypsy Kings song, which sounds like the word *Bomb!* or just shout 'Corporate whores!' at everyone shopping there.

My diary starts at Easter in 2011 . . .

Stage Two-Riding the Dog

Tuesday 17th April 2012 (Cornish date: 1973)

Cornwall

(Kernow Nothing)

Another week off work (on full pay), and it feels like I'm being made redundant really slowly. What's happened, for the first time in my life, is that the company I work for is having some financial problems, and they asked me (and some others) to take two weeks off work on full pay, which, theoretically, I can work back later at a beneficial rate (to me), as and when I want to. In fact they've said I don't ever have to work it back if I don't want to and they'll just take it out of my final salary, whenever that may be. Any overtime I do in the meantime will come out of what I owe the company, and when it's all paid back, I'll start getting overtime pay again. (This suits me fine as I don't ever do any overtime on principal.) This might be a precursor to unemployment, but I've never been told to go on holiday before. It's quite nice actually.

The weather has turned from last week's sunshine and higher temperatures to one of winter again, with hail and cold rain; more depressing as the hours drip by. The journey to California seems a million miles away and the idea of time to write, a fearsome one.

Went to my first comedy gig in Truro the other week and realised that either it was a shite gig or that I could easily make a living being a comedian. I'm depressed most of the time, and I could tell funnier jokes than the blokes I paid to see on stage. I'm not seriously thinking of an alternative career here, but watching the warm up, especially, was quite painful. I like to get drunk, I smoke, I'm not stupid—maybe there is something in the idea. We'll see if my real job goes to the wall.

This trip across America was fuelled by the NYC trip, when I realised how much I enjoyed the place, and although I knew that my experience so far was limited, I still reckoned this would be a worthy use of the best part of about three grand. When I first started checking online, the flights were about £265 return to NYC, which must have been a special offer of some sort, because by the time I got the money together and committed to buying them, the end cost was closer to £700. The cost cut into my budget, but in another remarkable turn of events, my work had just started giving out £500 bonuses every three months, so I could afford to still go. I ended up with a KLM flight (Royal Dutch Airlines), who's food was second to none, or so I was told by somebody called Patrick (who, it turns out, had no experience to call upon). It certainly looked good in the online write up.

This was my hoped for plan of action—fly to NYC (JFK), hang out in the city at my hotel (Hotel Carter, already paid for; £150 for two nights), meet up with the famous British rock'n'roll DJ Stuart Colman (the only person I actually vaguely knew in NYC at the time, from writing my previous book, Bass of Shades) for a coffee, natter etc., and then catch the Greyhound from the large, forbidding Port Authority bus station just around the corner from my hotel. Three and a half days on the coach with people who didn't want to kill or rob me (and didn't know I was carrying $2,500 in cash upon my poorly disguised, 6'4" white, English, middle class body). Change buses four times along the journey, plus many 'layovers,' where we had to vacate the bus for up to thirty minutes at a time and thus some kind of disaster was destined to occur along the way. Ending in Los Angeles, the city of angels, La-la Land, El Pueblo. After some online research, I found that the LA bus station, which we were to be deposited in at 7PM, was in a downtown area where I shouldn't walk around after dark, apparently (thanks guide books—don't think I'll read any more of them), and a taxi up to my Hollywood Hills residence was about $60 (including tip. Remember—TIP EVERYTHING!). Five nights in the Hollywood Hills in a house the Beatles apparently wrote songs in when playing at the nearby Hollywood Bowl. Meeting Ian Webber at some point (The bass player in my old college band and now a musician in LA. Sounds *better than it probably is; he seemed hyper-sensitive these days, and I didn't know how well we'd actually get on). See comedian Greg Proops record one of his fabulous podcasts live and then hopefully meet up with Mike Stax of* Ugly Things Magazine *who had just reviewed* Bass of Shades, *having a beer or two along the way. Any time left over would be used to concentrate on knocking* Roachville *into shape (the novel I was also working on). This could all just be an expensive waste of time really. I cursed myself for not being more proactive with the* Bass of Shades *book and getting a publisher to take it off my hands. Maybe Mike Stax would know someone out there who'd be interested.*

Anyway, Amtrak back to NYC, stopping and changing at Chicago for nine hours (the American government subsidises their railway service and yet, strangely, it is still efficient, clean, spacious, (obviously cheap), and yet hugely reliable—amazing, eh? How do they do it?). Finally, another couple of days in the Hotel (Get) Carter, enjoying the streets of the big apricot, until I jetted back with KLM to the traditional June sunshine of Heathrow airport. Topping and tailing the British legs of the journey with a lovely long National Express coach ride to and from Cornwall. (National Express? 50% bullshit if ever there was a name contest!)

[Our hero at rest]

Friday 18th May 2012

STILL CORNWALL . . .
(AND WHY NOT?—IT'S BRILLIANT!)

It's all coming on too quick. This journey is looming now, and as I expected, I'm starting to get cold feet. The first step in this journey of 12,000 miles and all that. It's gonna be fine, I keep telling myself; these things always are, but I'm thinking about Sam, Jess, and Ju now and what they'd do without me if anything went wrong and I didn't come back. Jess is three, and Sam is eleven years old. What will Jess remember of her father? How will Sam get through it if I didn't return? Ju will be missing me so much, but she's got a strong heart, and she'll always cope, eventually. We all would, in her shoes. I'm sure I'll come back, changed perhaps, but I'll come back. The leap into the unknown; it's a scary thing to do when your life is settled and predictable. The regret in later life, though, if I didn't take this opportunity, would tear me apart.

Twelve years down the line and I still think about the teaching job I had out in The Bahamas and what my life would've been if Sam hadn't arrived and I'd continued out there. I think I'm happier now than I would've been travelling around the world teaching, but all the places I'd have seen and the people I'd have met would've changed me from the man I am today, and my kids are everything. I'd not change a thing. They're the best thing I've ever done in my life. (I'd love to have two lives running parallel, though, just to see what would've happened.)

So it's a strange thing to do—to travel across America alone. I started to wonder if this was my mid-life crisis? I seem to have been having one for twenty years. When will it end, oh lord, when will it end?

This must've all been stupid nerves, but forty-five years on the planet and I was asking myself questions like:

'Was this really the time to pull yourself apart?' and

'Shouldn't I have mentally settled down by now?'

'Couldn't I have written at home?'

'Wasn't writing meant to take you away to another place?' (Hopefully I'd be at least able to answer that last question fairly soon.)

The weeks leading up to my departure had seen our bathroom mended and working again after a week without a bath or shower, the electric sockets in ours and Sam's bedrooms working once more, and my friend, Keith, making a start on clearing the bamboo from our wasteland of a garden. So the days were rushing past as I tried to focus on the experience that lay ahead. The details of the journey were all sorted but pushed to the background, niggling away in the back of my sleep-deprived mind. Working the nightshift can leave you feeling like you're permanently jetlagged as you try to interact with the real world of daylight hours and 'normal' life. Things slip past you, appointments are forgotten, and important information often needs to be repeated many times before it keeps its status. On one night, I was taking Patrick to a comedy club in Truro for the first time, and on another day, the Olympic torch was being carried through the streets of my local town of St. Austell. At some point, I meant to have a haircut, but I got the feeling that I may have missed the boat on that one. I liked to have everything planned out ahead, but it soon appeared that this was gonna be a 'skin of the teeth' experience, and I was not looking forward to being out of my comfort zone, regardless of my earlier bravado.

Everybody who knew about my plans told me how great an adventure it'd be, but 'everybody' wasn't doing it, and that may've been my problem with their advice. Could I deal with the loneliness and confusion with good natured grace? It seemed unlikely, when even an overly glued cardboard box containing fish fingers could annoy the fuck out of me.

I wondered if this trip itself could make a viable book? I should've checked with an editor by this point I suppose, but as I said, the days were slipping away from me.

Tuesday 22nd May 2012

CORNWALL
(MAKES EVEN YORKSHIRE LOOK CRAP)

Chatting with Keith today after he'd worked on the garden was great. He's such an excellent bloke. It took me back to when we used to hang out together twenty years ago. We spoke about our travels and philosophy. Still the same after all these years.

At this point, I was thinking more about how Jess would cope with me not being at home for a couple of weeks. In my mind, the poor thing would be so confused. I loved her so much that I missed her when I just thought about the trip. I hoped she didn't remember when she was older.

And Sam; she knew it was only for a couple of weeks, but I knew we we're close and it'd make her sad too. She was like my right hand. Which is probably why we knew how to get to each other so well. There's a bond there. We spent so much time together when she was first around. The apple of my eye. She'll always be my girl. I'm so proud of her. I hoped she'd remember the good times and not those stupid, shouty years that seemed to have taken the place of bedtime stories and cuddles. Growing up sucks.

Why was I doing this to myself (and to everybody else)? Why didn't I just cash in the dollars and stay at home, where it was comfortable, safe, and loving? I'm such a dick.

Thursday 24th May 2012

CORNWALL . . .

TO HEATHROW

(Fleeing the Country with the Dough)

The adventure begins. Come brave heart!—We must away to foreign lands where tales of greatness will be our currency, when once we do return to these shores. Let freedom be our watchword and the gods look upon our deeds with favour. AWAY!

I feel physically sick.

Just the thought of leaving my home and my family makes me slightly quiver. On more than one occasion I've told Ju that I didn't want to go, but she is resolute. Both she and Sam try to make me feel better, but if I could've gotten out of it, I probably would've.

(This is known as nerves. I hadn't experienced them before at this level. It fades in memory and with experience. Don't let it stop you—it didn't stop me).

I spent most of the last day at home on my own as Ju went to pre-school with Jess. Slowly, the hours drifted by. It was a boiling hot day too, so that didn't help. I washed and hung my two childhood teddies out on the line (Blue Bunny and Pink Bunny—no sexism in my house, even in the 1960s!). Forty-five years old, and all three of us still more or less in one piece.

Putting Jess to bed that night I wondered if I'd ever see her again, and it broke my heart.

But the time came for me to go. I'd ordered a taxi for 9.30PM, and I didn't want to have a tearful goodbye, so we hugged and kissed inside, and then I waited out on the roadside.

'Where are you off to then?' asked the taxi driver who usually dragged my drunken arse back from the pub of an evening.

'Los Angeles,' I replied.

'Los Angeles?!'

He wasn't expecting that. Then he asked me what I did, and I told him I was a writer, which pleased both of us I think.

At the bus station, I sat alone smoking a cigarette, looking at the still light, clear sky above St. Austell. It didn't seem real that I was about to start this ridiculous journey. But in twenty-four hours I'd be sitting in a bar in New York City, over three thousand miles away.

It was peaceful, apart from the odd drunken shout from girls at the local nightclub and the 'caw' of the seagulls that circled overhead. I sat with my legs outstretched and my small bag on the floor, contemplating my life. Within twenty minutes the coach turned up to start my journey, although as I climbed aboard I realised that this particular journey had really begun the day I returned from hitching to Paris back in 1987, some twenty-eight years ago.

Casual flashback ahoy!

I'd always regretted how that adventure ended. It had started out so well: I'd taken off to Paris and had been away for three weeks, met and befriended people along the way, lived the life I wanted, and yet took the easy option to return home with my parents when they came to visit. I should've gone grape picking in the south with Paul, but I was scared and lost my nerve. I regretted that decision for the rest of my life, and this whole thing may well have been a way to make it up to my earlier self. Again, I was scared, again, I tried to find reasonable arguments to take the easy option of staying at home, within the bosom of my loving family, but this time I had Ju, and she would hear none of it. I'd paid for the journey, and by god, I was going. I might be able to let myself down, but I couldn't do that to my beautiful Julie. The woman who'd put up with me for twenty years wasn't going to let me get away from this one.

So I boarded the nearly empty coach at 9.50PM and sat at the front. It started to get dark, but I realised that I wouldn't be getting much sleep here. The seats were uncomfortably upright and not designed for 6'4" sleepy gentlemen. We wheeled out of the streets of my home town and onto the roads that every minute took me further and further away from my comfort zone. Before we'd gone five miles, the coach hit an overhanging tree branch, which smashed off the passenger side wing mirror right in front of me. It was lost in the darkness that now surrounded us as we careered down a winding hillside. The driver started talking to me. In the still of the coach, it felt like everyone on board was listening and judging us on our responses. They probably had their earphones in, but I wasn't checking.

I'd been looking for omens for the last two weeks, trying to give myself ammo for backing out of this foolishness and here, in this clash of tree on coach, was another example. If you believed in tea leaf readers and the like, you could find excuses. I just sat back and thought how glad I was that I didn't own the bus. We trundled through the night visiting and picking up people in places I'd never heard of or seen before. I kept checking the clock on the bus, wondering how we'd make it to Heathrow on time (officially due in at 5.30AM).

Some people got off at Bristol airport and were then herded back on, because they weren't due to get off until Heathrow, some three hours later. People weren't getting on where they should, and others were trying to get off where they shouldn't. It was chaos. Like a British version of Ken Kesey's *Kool-Aid Acid Test*, but without the drugs or personalities. I stepped off for a couple of cigarettes when I could and even tried to sleep on board, but I couldn't have had more than a few minutes overall, due to the annoying design of the seats. So we visited Bath, Torquay, Reading, Teignmouth, Padstow, Bristol, and many other boring, fast asleep places on our journey, but eventually we did end up in Heathrow at the allotted time.

Friday 25th May 2012

HEATHROW TO

NEW YORK CITY . . .

(JET SETTING, GLOBAL SUPERSTAR)

I was first off, with my shoulder bag in my hand. It was my lifeline, and I'd have to keep it safe. All my paperwork and money was in there (bar about $1,000 cash in the lining of my jacket). I was due to fly from Terminal Four, which was miles away from the coach stop, so I set off walking. Now, the last time I was doing this particular journey was with Ju, it was Christmas time, and there were loads of other people around. It was all different at 5.30AM in the arse end of May 2012. There were only a few passengers around; most people had identity tags ('hang the lanyards, hang the lanyards . . .') hanging from their tired looking necks as they trudged like weary ants to their positions.

> *I remember lots of moving walkways two years ago, but now there are only two, and then you're presented with a free underground service to Terminal Four. It must be new, because the plastic is still clean and devoid of graffiti.*

We zipped along silently, bar the hum of electricity. (Another sign of newness—the tracks aren't misaligned so there is no 'clickity clack' sounds.) I looked at the empty carriages and wondered what I was doing here. Thoughts like that are designed for the early hours of the day. My flight wasn't due until 1PM, so really I had seven and a half hours to kill in Heathrow. Great. I did what any true Cornishman would do and headed for the bar.

Luckily for me, J D Witherspoon had got themselves in at the airport, and so at six in the morning, I ordered a black coffee and a pint of Abbot ale in the empty bar and started to wonder what I was going to do for the next few hours. I texted a few people, watched some shite Sky TV News without any sound on, listened to a bloke empty a couple of fruit machines, ate a couple of croissants, and had another couple of coffee/Abbot ale combos. I could feel the Abbot starting to take the edge off the day, so I stopped at three pints. I'd need to be aware of what was going on around me, as I had no-one else to rely on. The fat barman re-pinned the plastic Union flags strung from the ceiling back in place, and I wondered if they were there to celebrate the Queen's anniversary or just to welcome travellers from abroad. It was a dismal setting for a pub, with possibly the least atmosphere this side of outer space. It was like drinking in a branch of the Co-op Undertakers, but with slightly less jeu de vivre.

The day was turning into a scorcher as I stood outside smoking with the dirty and ashamed business men that always seem to haunt these moments. The odd youthful airport workers looked bored as their dirty fluorescent waistcoats soaked up the sun. This was in contrast to the gaggle of excited Japanese schoolgirl tourists across the road, who were obviously so glad to be standing in an industrial concrete, multi-story car park in a major airport in England that they could hardly contain themselves and took smiling photos of each other posing with obviously bored airport staff. One even filmed the others taking photos. The enthusiasm was so out of place, it was almost annoying. If it had been raining . . .

I went up to the departures area and had eight espressos to try and keep me awake. These were punctuated with cigarettes and people watching. Oh, the humanity of an airport! I then watched a fully grown man in brown corduroy lederhosen clasping a bunch of plastic flowers in one hand and his peaked cap (feather cocked to the left) in his other run by. Where he was going, I know not, but I pity the person he was running to meet.

The amount of luggage some people travel with is amazing. Their homes must be empty, judging from the size of the suitcases they wheeled around the terminal in ever decreasing circles. Children cried in frustration, burkas wandered past behind men pushing luggage trollies, directing their families on seemingly random tours of the facilities, and businessmen (those ever so important businessmen) stalked past, much as the prefects had back in school when their sense of superiority had been recognised. The rest of us minions' lack of direction left us people watching with espressos and cigarettes as the suits stalked towards a retirement in Surrey. And in this manner, I spent five hours of a sunny Friday in May 2012. What larks!

I had no luggage to put on the plane. I was travelling ultra-light with just my shoulder bag. Here's another one for you list fans.

Things that I took with me:
Black shirt x1
Black T-shirt x1
Black pair of socks x1
Ankle money-belt (unused)
Hay-fever pills x14
Passport
Copy of all paperwork relating to tickets
Hemingway's *A Movable Feast*
iPod touch 35G
iPod touch charger cable
American socket adapter for iPod
Mobile phone (+£10 credit)
Wash bag
Toothbrush
Hairbrush
Glasses case
My journal
Black Bic biro
$1,000 cash
50g Cutters Choice tobacco
Green papers x5
Sherbet lemons for flight
Los Angeles guide book
New York guide book

... and that was it. It all fit into my old canvas shoulder bag and gave me a few advantages, namely speed. I could move fast without bulky suitcases. Added advantages also included not looking like a tourist and not looking like I had any money or anything worth nicking. Being a solo traveller at the mercy of any given situation you find yourself in, blending in with your surroundings can save you a hell of a lot of trouble. And bearing in mind that I was planning to travel with almost the lowest of the low as an observer, it was a damage prevention exercise. I could always buy most things I needed along the way.

Eventually, I was allowed to go through the customs X-ray section and into the parade of 'designer name' shops and duty free bollocks that no-one with any sense ever passed a shekel towards. I've never been close to boarding an aircraft and suddenly discovered that I needed a new £850 sports watch, but if I had, I might not have cursed these pointless enterprises with such vigour. I mean, somebody must buy all this shit, or they'd go out of business. Perhaps it's the sheiks and Russian oligarchs that constantly fly in to buy football teams and great swaths of London town? All I know is that in Bergerac airport in southern France they have two chocolate bar machines, and that's your bloody lot.

All my paperwork was in order, I passed the metal detector test (my parents would be so proud of me), and went on my way. Trapped inside the system now, there would be no more cigarettes for over ten hours. The reception on the mobile phone would soon be gone too, so I sent out my last texts to Julie and felt so alone amongst the thousands of people surrounding me. Everyone seemed to be in a couple or a family. I couldn't look without becoming emotional and thinking about my own family. I tried to concentrate on the employees in the gaudy shops around me. A lady in the Burberry shop seemed to be staring at me (she probably wasn't), but I thought, 'Not even if I won the lottery would you be seeing any of my cash, darling.' I might not keep my finger on the fashion pulse, if there is such a thing, but even I know that Burberry is what dickheads wear.

Finally, my flight was open, and I wandered over to Gate 8, (another part of the airport with plastic seats and views of planes taking off). The sun beat in through the walls of glass, and I wished I was back at home constantly. I suppose you 'could' go back through airport security, but I've never heard of it before. Too late, I was the fly trapped in the web of civil airways. I was going nowhere. Well, not strictly true, obviously I was going somewhere, but just not quite sure where I wanted to be going. In many ways, that's true of most of us anyway, I guess.

The 'gate' filled up with my fellow passengers, and I tried to ignore them by reading Hemmingway's *A Movable Feast*, which was hard to concentrate on, due to the lack of sleep I'd had at this point (thirty hours since I woke up with Jess on Thursday morning) and, of course, the people talking total shite all around me.

After what seemed like eternity (and in fact, actually was eternity), the plane was refuelled, cleaned, rubbed down, and ready to be refilled with passengers. The rich and 'regular club' members were sent on ahead of us to test out the facilities on board, and when they were satisfied, we were allowed to take our own seats in steerage. I was luckily sat with a young couple who were nice enough not to annoy me with their personalities. The flight staff were efficient, and the pilot called us 'folks' in the richest American baritone you could ever hope to hear. Now that's what I call a reassuring voice. I imagine he sported a particularly spectacular moustache. Unfortunately, he was called Randy Stax or something, which slightly took the edge off the safety that his intonation had created. I imagined a wah-wah peddle going off somewhere in business class and Randy shouting, 'Oh Yeah!'

I tried to get back to Hemmingway and block out all the take-off crap. Zoom-a-tee-zoom and we were off the ground. We quickly rose to twenty nine thousand, nine hundred, and twenty-three feet, thirty-seven inches, and I started the process of giving myself neck ache by trying to sleep sitting up on a plane. It didn't work (again about twenty minutes in the whole flight). I asked for a single malt whiskey, as everyone around me took their complimentary cans of beer or little bottles of wine with their pretzels. They only had scotch and charged me £7 for the miniature (the cheeky fucks). That was the last thing I consumed on the flight. The food looked shit, and they had the nerve to come round more than once to offer us plastic cups of water. Water, for fuck sake? I paid the best part of £700 for this flight, and you're offering me fucking water? (And £7 whiskey miniatures?) Apart from the return journey, Delta won't be getting any more of my money, that's for sure. You'd expect this level of service from Ryanair or Easy Jet, but I thought KLM owned Delta. I expected BA or at least Virgin level of treatment. (Remember, last time I flew with Virgin they poured single malt from a bottle for me, and it was complimentary as often as I requested it (and request it, I did!)). To register my unhappiness, I refused to take the headphones that the brusque black woman was dealing out and had the TV screen turned off for the complete flight (although others enjoyed films I'd recently seen at work, such as *The Woman in Black* and *Mission Impossible 4*. I tried to concentrate on Hemmingway's words, but due to tiredness, I had to re-read them so often they made little sense.

Well, nothing ever happens when you're stuck on an aeroplane without a snake (although I did once have my fortune told on a 747 to Miami, which surprisingly turned out to be less than accurate), and as I didn't eat or drink anything else, I didn't need to move either. So seven hours later we land to a smattering of applause from behind me (I fucking hate it when people do that. Do they clap taxi drivers too? Twats.) and are herded out of the aircraft into the great American customs at JFK.

Last time I was here with Ju, this part of the experience took about two hours. This time, it was two minutes before I was at the desk. The security guy spotted the badge on my ratty old bikers jacket,

'Is that a Captain America pin?' And so then we had a slightly too long conversation about the recent films whilst he took photos of my eyes and fingerprints. (I think he was a being a bit forward for a first date.) I told him of my plans to see America from the Greyhound, and much like everybody else, his reaction was shock.

'You'll certainly see America from a Greyhound!' He alluded to great unpleasantness, and with a cheery, 'Good luck to you, sir,' he bade me on my way.

I didn't need to pick up any luggage and so was out in the taxi rank in less than twenty minutes from leaving my seat in the aircraft. The taxi was so hot I was sweating before we hit the tunnel checkpoint (still $6.50). I handed over the cash—my first purchase in the USA this year. (Funnily enough, the next time I visited New York three years later, I didn't have to pay anything.) It didn't cool down as we hit Manhattan.

It was 4PM on a Friday in the city that never sleeps, and gridlock was rife. The sun beat down, and American shoppers looked tired on their way home to watch *The Mary Tyler Moore Show*. I felt suddenly excited. Here I was again in New York City, a place I'd spent a great deal of my life walking around, inside my head. From the Spiderman comics I read as a kid to the gangster films I watched as an adult, this city had been the backdrop to all that was worthy and real. All my life I'd known New York, and here I was again. Two years ago, Julie and I had won a trip here, and it had blown me away, but this time I was alone, and yet I felt completely at home (as I often do in a big city). I suppose it's the anonymity I like. I wished Ju was with me, though.

The taxi, like everyone else, drove randomly, cutting lanes, indicating rarely, blaring the horn more frequently than was friendly, and we slowly edged closer to the Hotel Carter, where I was to stay for the next two nights. The tree lined, brownstone buildings with their outside steps, kids from *Fame* lounging everywhere in their jogging bottoms and sweat bands, metal fire escapes giving way to commercial buildings designed to display their gaudy content of machine guns and fat shakes. As we weaved, I marvelled at the American motors that surrounded our little, battered, yellow Mazda taxi. Even the trucks looked cool.

Hotel Carter on west 43rd Street, between 7th and 8th, is old, shabby, and in the heart of Manhattan (literally just off Times Square). It's had a murder and a fire in the last five years and is fabulously low rent. Like a time capsule from 1930, when it was opened under its original name 'Hotel Dixie' (whereupon the owners almost immediately went bankrupt). Several decades and nine various gruesome deaths later, the city decided to use it to house the homeless, and then finally, the public were invited back to rent the cockroach and bedbug infested rooms. It was crowned Trip Advisors 'Dirtiest Hotel in America' for four years in a row, from 2004 until 2008, and thus made the perfect base for me in New York City! All the Broadway shows are on the next block (not that that interested me), and the hotel has a very '60s Vegas feel about the place. From the street, thirty marble stairs lead up to the foyer, where a check-in can be executed. After paying the taxi the fixed-rate fare from the airport ($50 + tip), I joined the queue to sign in. They gave me Room 707 (on the 7th floor), and I stepped into the art deco elevator with a couple of other people. When I got out of the lift, I was in a building site. The hotel was being redecorated, I assume (and in quite a cheap way, judging by the lack of detail when applying the paint). I found my way to Room 707 expecting the worst and found it rather good actually. There was a large double bed, a chest of drawers, and a standard lamp to keep the thirty-two inch plasma TV company. A walk-in closet and a shower room completed the larger than expected room. The windows opened large enough for suicide, should the need arise, and the bathroom was well stocked with toilet paper, soap, shampoo, and towels. There was a vaguely working air-con unit wedged in one window, and although it was officially a non-smoking establishment, you could clearly sit on the window frame and smoke (as I did later, in the warm night air).

It was five o'clock US time (10PM GMT). I'd been travelling now for twenty-four hours, and I'd been more or less awake for thirty-nine hours. Clearly, now was the time to go out in search of beer.

Well, not exactly true; I went out in search of a nearby 7-11 that I was sure I'd located on the Internet last time I looked. I wanted to get some food inside me and pick up some toiletries I couldn't take through customs without luggage (aerosol cans and razors, etc.), but I couldn't find the store or just didn't have the energy to keep looking for it after half an hour. Luckily, I did find The New York Brewing Company bar and restaurant on West 44th, just across 8th Avenue. They had about thirty real ales on tap and fifty more in bottles. And it was happy hour (all pints $5). And I was happy.

I had three different pints from their extensive menu straight down (the watermelon was particularly memorable), met for the first time the wonderfully chatty Kara, and broke my veggie lifestyle with a cheeseburger and fries ($14), not leaving my seat at the bar once. I was in heaven, but my bones were in hell, and even though it was only around 6PM UST, I had to succumb to reality and crawl back to 707 and bed. I grabbed a bottle of water and a massive can of Budweiser from a small kiosk at the front of the hotel and had a cold, soap-free shower before flopping onto the bed. When I awoke at midnight for a pee, the city was strangely quiet. And again at 3AM. Eventually, I gave up trying to sleep and started to write, trying to record the details so far. This took me until 6AM.

Room 707's dirty old windows face out onto another building's sheer facade, and so there are no road noises to wake you, just the constant drone of some roof fans six stories below. I look down at them from my window and wonder if anyone has jumped from higher up the building onto them. There didn't appear to be any human being shaped dents in them, so I assume not. It is so hot, I sleep with the window open and don't wake until I need to.

Saturday 26th May 2012

New York City . . .

So it's 6.10AM in Room 707, and I have a short mission at some point—I will find that elusive 7-11. Although I did see a pharmacist sign, and I expect they'd have all I need anyway, I want to pick up some food and hole up here for a while. Two nights isn't really enough, to be honest (although I'm back in a week or so anyway). I could spend a week here quite happily wandering down to the New York Brewing Company bar and back, just writing in between.

There is no table and chair in 707, so writing can become painful on the neck and back after three hours, but that's small potatoes really. I shall definitely bring Ju here one day. It's not like the five-star hotel where we stayed last time by any imagination, but I think she'd be as happy as me.

A big eyed girl bummed a cigarette off me outside Hotel C last night just before I turned in. I stood up, my back against the building, leather jacketed, blue jeaned, Ramones T-shirted, not looking very touristy or lightly dressed. She sidled up to me, offering cash to buy a cigarette. I'd just that moment rolled one, so I handed it to her and pushed back the coins. She was polite, obviously a tourist, but well-mannered enough to clock me sometime later and say thanks again as she passed. I hoped she'd do the same for someone else.

The thing you get about New York City is how multi-ethnic it is. All nations seem to be working here, serving each other or just getting by. I mean, obviously, there's Chinatown, Little Italy, etc., but there's a hell of a lot of mixing going on too.

*I tried to send Ju a text last night, but I don't think my phone
can do that here. I hope they're all okay back at home. 6.25AM and
I miss them so much. I think the key to this is to keep busy and
not give yourself the time to dwell too much on stuff you can't do
anything about.*

The air-con unit that takes up a quarter of the window didn't
work too well. In fact, it didn't work at all, which is why the window
remained open all the time. In a perfect world everything would
be working, but in a typical human way, when technology lets us
down we resort to the easiest alternative. We retreat back through
knowledge at the drop of a hat, happy to reside in the past, where
once we understood the world. And thus, the window in room
707 remained wedged wide open, waiting for the next depressed
individual to squeeze past the knackered air-con unit and leap to
their death upon the rooftop blender below.

I know I mentioned it earlier, but is this the city that never
sleeps? I know Chicago is the windy city, and Los Angeles is the
city of angels (bit of a giveaway, that one). Where I come from in
Cornwall we only have one city, and that's just called 'Truro.' It
doesn't get a job description like in America. Perhaps The Cobbled
City of Bollocks might be considered, or perhaps The Small Pasty?
I dunno, but it's not as exciting as The Big Kumquat, that's for sure.

Oh shit. I forgot to mention, a few shops up from the New York
Brewing Company is Birdland. The actual 'bird land'—home of
the birds. Tweet city central. No, actually it's named after Charlie
Parker, the great jazzer who revolutionised the music scene and
lived not too many blocks away. He was nicknamed 'Bird,' because
he wore a gingham dress and lived in a nest. I guess that this was his
actual club, because it's apparently a sacred place for jazz fans and
could be considered the mecca of many things known as cool, trad,
and bebop. I shall try and go there tonight I think. It's not cheap to
get in, but I think it'll be worth it.

Here's some guff about the history of the place that explains the
Birdland I'm talking about. Much like The Cavern Club back in
Liverpool, it turns out that it isn't the original one and appears to
be more of a money making exercise than a cool historical venue.
America doesn't handle its own history very well (or its present).

And disappointingly, Charlie Parker wasn't even a transvestite.

"When the original Birdland opened sixty years ago in December, 1949, Charlie Parker was the headliner and the club was located on Broadway, a block west of the 52nd Street scene, which was a hotbed of jazz in the 1930s and 40s.

"In addition to Bird, many jazz legends were regulars at the club. Count Basie and his smokin' big band made Birdland their New York headquarters, eventually recording George Shearing's "Lullaby of Birdland" live at the club. John Coltrane's classic Quartet regularly appeared at the club in the early 1960s, recording "Live at Birdland." And the famous DJ, Symphony Sid Torin, made a name for himself broadcasting live from the club to radio listeners up and down the eastern seaboard.

"Considering the excitement that Birdland generated on a daily basis, it's no surprise that the club attracted its share of celebrities. Regulars to the nightly festivities included such household names as Gary Cooper, Marilyn Monroe, Frank Sinatra, Joe Louis, Marlene Dietrich, Ava Gardner, Sammy Davis, Jr. and Sugar Ray Robinson.

"But as a new popular music, Rock & Roll emerged, Birdland's fortunes declined in the 60s and its doors were closed on Broadway and 52nd in 1965. After many 5 am nights, the club needed to take a nap.

"Birdland awoke uptown in 1986 at 2745 Broadway, on the corner of 105th Street where it was well renowned for its great acoustics and unique setup.

"Now, half a century later, the Birdland banner has been reborn in midtown and called, "close to perfection for serious fans and musicians," by The New York Times.

"Since the re-emergence of the club, midtown Manhattan has been treated to some of the best jazz on the planet, including memorable sets by such musicians as Oscar Peterson, Pat Metheny, Diana Krall, Dave Brubeck, George Shearing and Tito Puente"—so says the club's website, birdlandjazz.com

So I'm lying on the bed, stark naked (it's really hot), listening to jazz (it's really cool) on the iPod that's wired precariously into the mains socket (it's really dangerous) at the foot of the bed on a Saturday morning in New York City. This is a movie, right?

I need a black coffee and a cigarette or three. Its 7.42AM now, and I've been up since 3AM writing. I need to check out that chemist too, but I'm not going sightseeing. I should pick up some postcards and send them today at some point too. Tourist crap is easy to find

*around here because we're so near to Times Square. I'll pick Sam
and Jess something up on the return leg of the journey, when I'm
back in town in a couple of weeks.*

The sweat rolls off him, and with every bead that crawls down
his arm or falls from his brow, a portion of his strength leaves him,
until soon he has none at all and is only good to fall naked upon a
bed and sleep until it returns from whence it left. He's done nothing
to create this situation; the weather has conspired to destroy him,
and his body provides the decoration of decay as it lays spread-
eagled upon the sheets in the afternoon sunlight. (Bit of literature
there, for all you highbrows.)

Eventually, I left the room and went in search of a coffee for
breakfast, but first to Duane Reade, the pharmacist, to find a nail file,
shampoo, and hairspray. I forgot I needed toothpaste, but I don't
think they would've had it anyway. It really wasn't that kind of shop.
In fact, I've never been in a shop claiming to be a pharmacist that
was less useful; rows upon rows, over two floors of perfume, make-
up, and beer(!), but not a tube of bloody toothpaste to be seen. I
left, confused and furry of teeth. Then I bought some postcards and
stamps from a corner shop that appeared to sell more electric goods
than tourist tat. 'Ten for a dollar,' it said outside on the carousel,
but with them charging two dollars for a $1.05 stamp, it ended up
at $23! I think there's a city tax thing they add at the till that rises
the more touristy you sound. To bring a little karma into the world,
they'd locked the stamps in a drawer and lost the key, so they had to
take a power drill to the thing. After about ten minutes of watching
the worst safe crackers in NYC at work, they'd finally destroyed
their own counter and handed me my five stamps. It was hard to
keep a straight face. I picked up some random toothpaste from a
newsagents and went back to the hotel, deposited the toiletries,
and wrote up the postcards to send as soon as I spotted a blue post
box. Back outside for a cigarette and then on to seek out the Port
Authority bus station, a block away down 8th Avenue at 42nd
Street. It was a dirty, great black building giving off bad vibes on a
street full of white stone and glass fronted shops. I found out where
I had to go tomorrow and, fearing for my soul, went back to the
New York Brewing Company (NYBC) for a cooling beer. Damn.
It was shut. So I ended up in Smiths bar and grill on the corner of

44th and 8th. Its most famously a backdrop in the film *Taxi Driver*, and it hasn't changed a bit. One side is a bar and the other a booth-ed eating establishment with a wall of glass doors that they slide away on sunny mornings. It looks, and feels, timeless when you're in there sitting on the tall bar stools getting a cold drink served by Mike the barman, a welcoming host. He looked like Woody but spoke like Sam from *Cheers*.

A couple of beers there, a cigarette outside or two, and then a full Irish breakfast at 10.30AM . . . followed by another beer, before heading down to the NYBC for a final one. I kept looking for a post box, but there were none that I could find—it was all litter bins and jogging, healthy-types mixed in with gangly tourists and fat locals complaining. The blacks kept advertising parking spaces by waving flags at the oncoming cars or trying to sell tickets on buses for tourists to tour the city highlights on open top red London buses. I crawled off to a sweaty sleep in the lunchtime heat. All I wanted was relief from this damned heat, and all I found was more sunshine. People banged doors outside my room to wake me up when I fell asleep, and I rolled over to defeat them, when I heard sounds of animals.

Birdland is charging thirty dollars tonight to hear an hour and a half of jazz from someone I've never heard of's 'Five.' It feels like a lot of money for an hour and a half of entertainment (plus drinks). I shall have to contemplate.

> *I've had a hot shower and shampooed my hair. I'm not sure I feel normal in this weird movie I seem to be in, but I feel cleaner. I'm contemplating having a cigarette by the window, as there doesn't appear to be any smoke detectors and the window opens enough to get a body out of it, if need be. The air feels humid outside, but not the tropical heat I've had in the Bahamas. This is humid and dirty, like a dusty attic that has just showered. You feel oppressed on the street, and movement becomes a chore. There should be more seats outside so you could sit and watch the other fools pass.*
>
> *Hours move slowly here. It's probably the thickness of the air. The humidity has made 1.30PM take three hours to reach 2.30, and I don't know, at this rate, if I'll ever see tomorrow.*

The chest of drawers in the hotel room had inlaid wood around each drawer and fancy handles on each of the four drawers. It was clearly too good for a hotel that also displayed a print on the wall with paint splattered on the glass (as if the decorators hadn't bothered to remove it from the wall as they painted). A 'strange mix' was the forte of this establishment, although the majority of guests that I saw looked on the disappointed side of happy and the regular side of weird. My leather biker's jacket was worn alone, a symbol of original thought in a cotton top world of amazement.

Eventually, I decided to phone home and went down to the attached kiosk that sold water outside, looking for some quarters for the payphones in the street. The guy sold me a phone card instead for five dollars, which had a hundred minutes of credit on it for international calls.

'It'll save you loads, man. The pay phones will eat your quarters and only give you a minute or two.'

I tried it back up in 707 on the hotel phone, and he was right, but by the time I rang home it had gone 9PM GMT, and so I only spoke to Sam and Ju. It was good to hear them, and I think Ju was especially pleased (I rang again the next morning to speak to Jess). It was hard. I could hear the emotion in Ju's voice; she was missing me as much as I was her.

Back to Smiths bar for some food, but it was full by now, so I had a Bud and then back to the NYBC for some chips and a couple of beers. I got chatting to the barmaid again and found out she was only on five dollars an hour working from 11AM until midnight. Once I'd made sure she didn't have to share her tips, I tipped big. Kara Tabor (for it was her) then gave me the two beers for nothing when I asked for the bill. She stood and chatted about life for ages and was really friendly, used the word *awesome* a bit too much, she was reading using a Kindle, and was a fan of Stephen King. Kara was moving in with her boyfriend in a week or two and came from the Midwest, where her dad was a salesman, so they had all moved around a lot. I promised to pop in and see her when I got back from LA, and because she's interested, I'll drop the free copy of *Ugly Things* with my book reviewed in it that I'm due to get out in there (I've already paid for two copies at home anyway).

'Ever thought of writing movie scripts?' she asked in passing at one point.

'Not interested,' I bluntly replied with half a smile.

'Oh, I suppose that makes sense.'

I didn't want to burst her bubble, but although she wants to be an actress and is self-aware enough to say that she has a nice smile and is always happy, I'm British, old enough to be her father, and looking at reality from the shitty end of the telescope. Still, her enthusiasm was nice, like an encounter with a spaniel puppy.

It rained while I stood outside to have a cigarette, and I watched the theatre crowds slide up and down the sidewalks. I decided not to give Birdland my money today and went back to my room to shower off the sweat and watch some stupid television. I tried to sleep from 9PM onwards and got it better than recently, waking at 2AM.

Sunday 27th May 2012

New York City . . .

(THE AVERAGE SIZED PIECE OF FRUIT)

Probably the last day I'll be able to write until Los Angeles, what with being on the bus for the next few days. I've got until twelve noon in the hotel room and then until nearly midnight before I get on the bus. The mission today is—post postcards post haste, get the ticket for the Greyhound, find out where I catch the bus, and finally, if I can find that elusive 7-11, I'll grab some food and water for the journey west.

It started to rain heavily outside the hotel room window. The large splats on the window sill suggested to me that my sunglasses may not get much use. By 7AM, I needed a coffee and a cigarette (I'd been up on the phone to Cornwall since 4AM) and was still a little out of wack with New York City. Today's Greyhound journey west would add another couple hours onto the time difference, but at least it would be more gradual and my body clock would be able to accept it better. Much as I love flying nowadays (and I really do enjoy the ludicrousness of defying gravity in a metal tube surrounded by insanely flammable liquid), the one drawback is the jetlag. It always gets to me because I just can't sleep on flights, and it debilitates me for days.

Here's some news for you: sport is a big thing here. Apparel for sale everywhere, shows on the flat screens in all the bars; it seems to define some people in a way that isn't so overwhelming back in the UK. Every bar shows sport, although why beer consumption is so heavily linked with baseball is beyond my limited intelligence. At least at home you can drink without 100% sport in your face all the time. I'm depressed enough without having the physical prowess of superior human beings shoved down my neck with the mind numbing beer as a psychotic chaser.

By 8AM I still need a coffee and a cigarette.

So I went out, creature of habit that I am, to Smiths bar for breakfast (a full Irish was thirteen dollars, including black coffee and untouched water—'The only free thing in New York,' said Chris, the waiter on my first visit). The bar part was shut until 12 noon (it was Sunday), but the food side was doing good trade. It seemed from the accents that most of it was from the UK... typical. I can't stand it when I'm out of the country and I hear an English accent anywhere; it drives me nuts. The booths were full up, so I shared the floor space with a fat Glaswegian, his partner, and the back of a Geordie's red, lumpy neck. The front windows and wall of the bar were slid open to the sidewalk outside, and finally some locals were walking in and taking seats. The place started filling up as I headed out to the pharmacist to pick up some nuts for my journey west, then back to the hotel room. Sitting in the 707, my bags filled and ready to go on top of the unmade bed, I tried to watch some of the telly, but my concentration levels were gone as I constantly checked my watch. The minutes of the last hour crawled away and hid until I was dragged screaming from the room. Loaded down with my belongings, I finally posted the postcards in the hotel's own letterbox, which I hadn't even noticed before. Then I checked out.

Great—midday on a sunny Sunday in New York City. Ten and a half hours to kill and no desire to do anything touristy. I head out onto the streets without looking back at the black cab drivers sitting on the fenders in groups yakking as loud as possible:

'YO! FRANKIE! WHATS 'APP'NING?'

No-one ever replies to that question.

I walk on.

All the black kids wear white clothes that look brand new. All the white kids try to look like black culture is really their thing. Their clothes all look like they've been through a cycle or two.

I go to the Greyhound section of the ticket office in the Port Authority on 8th Avenue and completely screw up their system, needing a nearby member of staff to help me with their self-service ticket machine. Defeating the whole point of the exercise, a black girl in a fluorescent jerkin prints out my ten tickets and a two-ticket itinerary that illustrates the times and places of my upcoming bus changes. It doesn't say what other stops we'll be making or how many times I'll have to step out of the bus for it to be cleaned, filled with fuel, and a new driver installed that will need to see everybody on board's tickets all over again, but I'm sure I don't need to know that just yet anyway. She places them neatly in a little blue folder and hands it to me with a, 'Have a nice journey,' coming out of a face that screams, 'Fuck you, asshole!' I do prefer it the other way around. I am an asshole who needs someone to help him touch a touchscreen ticket machine.

Everywhere I go, I see black people in the service of everyone else. I'm middle class and white; I feel worse about this than I do about the starving millions in wherever. Maybe it's because it's in my face, maybe it's just so obvious. This shit: greed, power, status bollocks. I'm too involved. I've been a pan washer; I've stacked shelves; I've been elbows deep in pigswill. It doesn't make you a better person earning a shitty wage, it just makes you hate the people who don't have to do it. And when they look down at you (and they always do), you could cut out their cold dead hearts. No compassion, you see? No compassion equals no humanity, so it's not really murder. You can't murder a carrot, can you?

So it's 12.30. Do I want to walk a long way from the Port Authority, as I'll only have to walk back carrying all my stuff.

(Oh, that's weird. As the writing crosses the page, the ink looks like it's running out of this pen, as I lie with my head on my arm on the left of the page.)

Obviously I look for a bar.

I want to drink in a bar called Dave's Bar in Hell's Kitchen, but I pass it twice, and it remains closed. I stand and watch a soup kitchen van hand out free food under a sign for the Lincoln Tunnel and the watchful eyes of New York's finest as they sit in their cruisers opposite, drinking takeaway coffee and eating pastries. The down and outs queue in the sunshine, a few umbrellas up to protect the older ones from the harsh sun. All of them look dirty and homeless (although they probably aren't all homeless), and all of them are either black or Hispanic. The only white face I see in the crowd of fifty or sixty is a woman in a clean white shirt, black pants, a clipboard in one hand and a gesticulating finger in the other poking holes in the air above the people's heads. I can't hear what she's saying from this distance, and at first I assume it's about forming a good line to receive their carrier bag not even half filled with some food, but after a couple of cigarettes, I realise she's spouting a Sunday afternoon sermon at these poor fucks. As if they haven't suffered enough. For a second there I was going to go over and offer to give some money to help, but when God came to town, I turned away and walked down the sun dappled, tree lined side streets to a bar.

The House of the Brews on West 51st and 8th, looking for all the world like a New York version of that famous Cheers bar; a walk down, basement bar with practically no external lighting drew me like a leather jacketed moth to its flame. Down some steps into a cellar lit by neon wall signs and strip lights, long and low. I nearly doubled the cliental as I put my bag down, hung my leather on the back of the stool at the solitary window end of the bar, ordered a Guinness, and turned to watch a Led Zep live video playing on a screen behind me. A young couple ordered some food, and I noticed the man look me up and down when he heard my accent. I didn't fit in anywhere. Cut off sleeves on my old Ramones Aid T-shirt, black and grey hoodie tied around my waist, blue jeans, and steel toe-capped trainers. My greying hair was long and swept back; my stubble stuck through the glistening skin on my face. When the pint turned up I went outside for a cigarette. The world was doing fine out there, so I returned to my seat. The pint fell down my throat, and I ordered another. The barmaid was friendly and quite nice on the eyes; she had an Emma Peel gene somewhere in her make-up. It was a dark bob, black dress/shirt, nice smile, 5'5" tops, and older than you'd expect, possibly thirty-five? It's really hard to tell after a certain age, and frankly, in a cellar bar the lighting suits all of us over a certain age. I may have sat too near to the window.

I went outside for another cigarette. The sunshine was still making me sweat and yet the clouds were building up. I watched a classic red American fire engine wander down the side street. This sleepy side lane was working its ass off to sell Thai and Chinese food across from me. There was Russian food beside the bar and hotels up high steps from the sidewalk, where the chefs sat as the afternoon continued. I went back inside for the third Guinness. This was not a long game, but Guinness is 4.3%, so I reckoned it could be a session beer today. So far, no trips to the toilet downstairs and I'd outstayed people after me who'd arrived, eaten, and gone. I was now a local fixture. I asked the barmaid how much the Guinness was.

'$7 something,' was the answer.

Cheekily, I asked if it was cheaper if I bought in bulk? She replied that if I ordered a fourth, it'd be on her.

I ordered a fourth pint of Guinness.

This was going okay.

'Why is it,' I pondered out loud, 'that this pint tastes so much better than the others, I wonder?'

Her reply wasn't as impressive as I'd hoped for. I felt a bit disappointed.

'Maybe it's because I paid for it.'

'Oh yeah, that'll be why.'

Okay, so she didn't do witty banter. No matter. Oh look, I'm outside again having a cigarette or two as soldiers and sailors stroll by in their finest togs. Families of happy, affluent little Americans stroll by in the peaceful Sunday sunshine. Is that a sliver of dog shit beneath your nostril, sir? No, apparently I don't fit in, what with my attire and the smoking thing. It's not even a real cigarette, darling, he's smoking tramp butts.

I notice a guy on the street next to me in a uniform looking a bit like Bill Murray. He's been there since I turned up, but I realise he's working, so I looked the other way. His job is to entice passing members of the public into a Russian food establishment. He's called Gjoni. We shake hands. He's from Latvia or somewhere, (sorry, Gjoni, if you're reading this; I was starting to blur around the detail edges by the time we spoke). We had a long conversation about which I remember nothing, but I know, even now, that we are absolutely best friends. I will always hold Gjoni the best of men.

He was a few years older than me (fifty something), about the same size of body as me, and reminded me of an old friend of mine called Austin with his demeanour. And after all, he came over to me to talk, so what's not to like?

I returned to the bar, where pint number five was settling as two army boys came in and sat next to me. Sergeants, judging from the stripes on their crisp, brown uniforms (and confirmed later in conversation). They were youngish, no older than twenty-five at a push. As one departed to talk on his phone, I engaged the nearest in conversation.

Do you see what's happened? Five pints of Guinness has affected my ability to shut the fuck up in public. Without realising it at this point, I may have actually been drunk. I'm certainly quite charming and witty (that should've given the game away). I ask lots of exciting questions, and all goes well. His pal returns and at no point do either of them call me a total and utter cunt, so I deduce that I didn't get all argumentative, but stuck to my supportive, understanding, we're-all-in-this-together attitude and cruised on past any potential stormy weather. It was all light banter. Rick and Richard (really?) were cool chaps (even if their jobs involved killing people and getting a wage for doing it every month). I even bought them a round of drinks (that they never reciprocated—the bastards!). Then they left the bar. I went back outside and had another couple of cigarettes and another chat with Gjoni but was quickly back on the stool for pints six and seven. I asked the barmaid what her name was and when she finished her shift.

'Alison, and eight.'

'That's a funny surname,' I said to no-one in particular and got the response it deserved.

I told her about the English pub concept of buying drinks for any staff that take our fancy or do an exceptional job, as opposed to the American way of tipping a dollar for every order delivered as requested. I talked about how I'd worked behind the bar myself and then ordered my eighth pint of Guinness. It was now 7.35PM, and I still had three hours to wait for my bus. Alison agreed to have a drink with me at the end of her shift. I stressed it was just a drink and that I was a married man, showing her my wedding ring. I wear it proudly and am not offering sex to anyone I talk to or enjoy the company of. (Gjoni breathed a sigh of relief somewhere up on the street!) Yeah, I flirt, but that's okay; it's only a bit of fun. Nothing will, or has, ever happened since I met my wife—twenty-one years of totally happy monogamy, thank you. Honestly. I am not bullshitting! I've seen good looking women, sure, I've spoken to a few, I've bought a couple drinks and generally been over-generous with my tips, but I have never considered going with anyone but my best girl. Some people don't believe this. Whatever. I know the truth, and those that matter know it too.

Now back to the shagging.

So what happened next? Well eight o'clock wandered off as I sat at the bar, hopeful that I'd be able to buy Alison a drink and have a proper, uninterrupted conversation with her. I'm not sure what happened next (remember, eight pints of Guinness down), but Alison continued talking and working. I paid my tab ($75+), left the prerequisite tip, left the bar without my half-smoked tobacco pouch, didn't get my conversation with Alison, and gave Gjoni fifty dollars as well for no good reason other than he was a good man and I was drunk and flush at this point.

I headed for the Port Authority station to catch my Greyhound dream at 10.30PM. I was two hours early. I was completely drunk. I was also completely lost. I walked in the vane hope I'd just come across the place, but after a while, I was completely done in, so I climbed into the back of a taxi and asked him to just take me there.

He pointed out that the location was just around the corner. I pointed out that I was completely drunk and that I'd never make it. I knew me. I'd never find the place without his help. He realised a safe sale and drove me around the corner. I got out of the cab less than two minutes after I'd got in, paid the small fare with a large tip, and walked unsteadily up the steps and down the escalators of the Port Authority bus station, ending up at Gate 78 to catch the bus west. There were already some people there waiting an hour and a half before we were due. I wandered outside for some smoking activity. When I came back inside, the queue had got bigger and the folks didn't look at all like me. I didn't speak more than a word or two at this point, just laughed at the delays, the anger around me, and the advert that was sat next to us saying, "This is the future of bus travel." We were half an hour late getting on the bus, and I lay on the floor of the bus station just watching the chaos. Hey, I was the real traveller amongst all these people; they were only going a few hundred miles down the line. I'd already travelled three thousand miles just to get to this point, and I had another three thousand to go. What was half an hour to the likes of me? I didn't even have luggage to store under the bus—I was super light. Eventually, in the dark, I got on board, found a seat to myself a few from the front, and sat on my first ever Greyhound bus. Woo Hoo! (as they say), but be aware that I was now, actually right now, living the bloody dream, pal. What lay ahead was unknown.

Obviously, I was the only white person on the half-full coach. I was also the only non-American (okay, 'English,' if you must) and certainly the only drunk person on board. Luckily, I am a great drunk and therefore fell asleep as we pulled out of NYC in the Sunday darkness of nearly midnight. And so the journey begins. The game is afoot. (Especially, if you play twelve inch poker.)

Monday 28th May 2012

New York City (NY)
[NOT YELLING]

Richmond (VA)
[VERY AMERICA]

Winston-Salem (NC)
[NAUGHTY CLIVE]

Knoxville (TN)
[TINY NIGEL]

I had two packets of nuts and raisins to eat along the way and a bottle of water (two to three dollars, depending where you bought it). This is all that I had bought for a three-day journey, on the basis that there must be places to grab a bite from along the way. Surrounding me on the bus were the most bizarre creatures of the night. In front, a fat middle-aged black woman; behind, oh yes, they had that in handfuls, my dear nervous reader!

It was both fascinating to watch and satisfying to know that however bad life was or could ever get, my arse would never look that bad. Leopard print leggings, animal print shirts, nylon when they should be cotton. Remembered when I wish they were forgotten. I kept my mouth shut and kept all comments to single word answers,

55

if I was questioned (it's a lot harder to define an accent if the person doesn't use sentences). I tried to doze and did get a bit in, but the bus stopped for 'rest stops' every two hours, and I got off each time to have a couple of cigarettes. Some people left the bus at these 'rest stops' before we made Richmond (VA) at 5.30AM. The rest of us had to unload, get off, loiter (smoke a cigarette) for the best part of an hour while Greyhound got us another bus and driver.

It gets light early at this time of the year (you can see shapes by 4AM), and so, when the new coach turned up, it was easy to see that it was an old knackered beast and certainly not 'the future of bus travel.'

People were waking up, and some knew each other, so there were conversations and 'clicks' being created all around me. I continued to keep my own council and sipped water between cigarettes outside the Richmond bus station.. With so much time to kill, I went into the café and had a coffee.

By 6.30AM we were back on the road, burning the miles up in a most leisurely fashion. The speed limit varies depending where you are (up to 75mph), but most of the coaches seemed to peak at around 60mph on a good day. Everything overtook us, and I began to feel three and a half days to LA may be a little optimistic of Greyhound. I think I saw a bicycle go past us at one point. (Actually it was two bicycles in the back of a black pickup.)

More little stops, more cigarettes out in the sunshine, more recognition of faces on our little bus. Still no conversations with a large white male smoking funny hand-rolled cigarettes (that's me).

The next change of bus was at Winston-Salem (NC). At this point in the journey, I'm still looking for confirmation from any professionals on hand that I'm in the correct queue and have the correct time. This involves a great deal of standing around watching other humans buying tickets, listening to them talking crap and yet asking smarter questions than me. (But, hey, I was a virgin to all this—they must've all been on at least a thousand trips with Greyhound.) Nobody gives me any grief, no-one intimidates anyone else, the closest I get to altercation is when someone asks for a light or tries to bum a fag for money.

Back on the new bus in Salem and our new driver is a nice fella, full of gentle asides and comments. A big black woman gets on at the next stop and avails herself of half of my seat. I have no idea what she's resting her other buttock on, and I'm not about to ask. We pertinently ignore each other throughout our time together, although at one point, out of the blue, she pokes me in the ribs and offers me a fruity sweet, which I turn down (well, she looks like she needed it more than I did).

You could see alliances form between people of similar backgrounds as the loud, mouthy gits sat with their audiences and the quiet, mousey types pulled their seat belongings a little closer. It was all bragging and use of the terms *hos, bitches,* and *down with my home boys* from both sexes (which surprised me). I suppose the gang culture is so rife in a society that is built so heavily on status and your position in the pecking order that it's mimicked at all levels of society. The untouchable 'white house' figure is the bus driver. They are gods. No-one argues; no-one questions their opinions. Mostly they get treated like some bizarre holy figures. If someone pisses off a Greyhound driver for anything, they will surely rue the day. At the start of each journey, each new driver introduces him or herself to the waiting faithful. Spouting words from the good book *Grey*, chapter; *Hound*, paragraph; have a nice day. They repeat the mantra of dos and don'ts and do not appreciate shouted out comments. Heckling the driver will get you a stern response that may even find you left by the roadside. You have no say in that; the driver's word is law around these parts. I watch as people try to butter up different drivers along the journey, trying to align themselves with these power centres like the weedy, needy followers of a bully. I find it hard to watch these cheerleaders fall at these driver's feet, but fall they do. Christ, I even hear a round of applause break out when we make a station on time. Now, in the UK that would be taken as a sarcastic comment from a bus load of people, but over here they really mean it. Well done, no really well done, for doing what we've all paid you to do.

Monday continues, and the road takes us onto our next change of bus and driver in Knoxville (TN). At 6.30PM we crawl into the bus station for a twenty minute layover, where we get to meet our new leader. That'll be the fourth bus today, and we're only on day one!

We're outta there in half an hour, and our new (old) bus (we don't see another newish bus in the whole journey after leaving NYC behind) is just eight hours away from being in our past. Lucky really, because my seat is cramped, not really secure (it bloody wobbles for fuck sake!), and uncomfortable. Luckily, I get to share it with an old Mexican woman, who puts the arm rest down in the middle of the seat between us, after poking me in my ribs, as if I'm going to molest her or something. She's obviously disappointed that her arm rest coy ploy didn't get me going, because she later offers me a pretzel and calls me 'sir.' This humble display gets a typically British, stiff upper lipped 'no, thank you' response, and I return to staring resolutely out of the window. In the whole journey, I always get the window seat (by choice), and so I watch as the America of my television screen is laid out before my eyes. Like playing an internal game of eye spy, I tick off items as I see them, 'Oh look, there's the metal farm wind generator thing, or oh look, there's a Dunkin' Donut sign. What's that? It's a bloody great rig of an American truck drivers association member overtaking us. Oh. My. God!' It's at this point I get my first sighting of Route 66, just after the coach is overtaken by two trikes with female passengers turning to wave at us as they pass. I put my hand up to the window and felt like a tool, but I did it anyway, caught up in the moment. The trikes overtook us and then skipped back onto Route 66, which ran beside us on the right, slowing down on the rough, old tarmac. We passed them, but I wished I was with them and not 'riding the dawg.'

This may be the point that a new dream started to build about doing the Route 66 ride with Keith on a couple of bikes. In fact, it was at this point that I started to enjoy the journey, as I remembered our conversation in my back garden. I realised that it was all going to happen, and I'd better try and feel it in the here and now.

I started to hear conversations from the back of the bus about passengers being ex-felons and how they were going to pick up their boyfriends, who were being let out in a day or two. The level was set, until I distinctly heard mention of someone placing his gun down on his wallet to illustrate that:

'That bitch was getting no more of my money, man. Ha ha.'

So I was clearly the least armed or incarcerated member of this passenger list. (Greyhound rules are explicit that no guns are allowed on board, however, as one driver later on wanted to tell us in her introduction speech, but of course, at this stage I was still a novice and could be rattled by this casual gun reference.) Then the drug boasting started. Oh yeah, they'd had 'em all, and to extreme measures. That's why they were covered in tattoos and looked like the lower end of trailer trash, whilst bigging themselves up to unquestionable levels. For people who could only just afford the bus fare, why did they think anyone would believe they could afford high quality drugs that weren't ninety-eight per cent cleaning product? Bragging the loudest was a thin, white, skater boy with long, dreadlocked hair and the complexion of a corpse.

'Oh, my mom. She is so beautiful. She's crazy. She's fifty-one but acts sixteen. She let me do what I wanted. She was drunk all the time. I just did everything . . . ' he tailed off.

He was so worldly wise, he'd seen it and done it all before, you'd even have thought what 'it' might be. And all the girlies thought he was pretty fly for a white prick. I thought he was annoying when I first saw him, then he opened his mouth. After ten minutes, I wanted to stick his stupid head down the onboard toilet and flush it until he stopped moving.

'Oh yeah, I got that ADH. I can't sleep. Oh yeah, I'm on it.'

He'd have been on the end of my steel toe capped boot, if I'd had my way by now.

It starts to get dark outside, but the comfort breaks continue throughout our journey, roughly every two hours. It's not much of a comfort. I merely smoke a couple of cigarettes and slurp at my water. The one advantage to this diet is that I don't need the toilet, which is an important bonus on a coach with no loo.

Back on the road, the car lights zip past my left-hand side, their reflection in the coach windows gives the impression that we're driving through the middle of two opposing lanes of oncoming traffic. Separating the stream of light, we carve our way westward towards Memphis tomorrow at 2AM.

Tuesday 29th May 2012

MEMPHIS (TN)
[TINY NIGEL]

LITTLE ROCK (AR)
[ANAL RUPTURES]

AMARILLO (TX)
[TERRY'S XYLOPHONE]

In Memphis (TN) at two o'clock in the morning, we had a forty minute layover, and as I sat smoking outside in the hot summer night air, a white, long haired, bearded bloke sat next to me. He had a long face, was younger than me, and asked if he could have one of my cigarettes. No problem. We fell into easy conversation about smoking, music festivals, and life in general. He hadn't been on our bus, but was joining it from here for a few stops, hoping to end up in Oklahoma in a day or two. Eventually, he wandered off to sort out his ticket and I was left alone with a young black bus station worker, who also scabbed a fag off me but had to watch as I rolled it for him. He was cool, though, and full of friendliness. Possibly the essence of youth running through his veins, but I like to think it was more a case that this was actually his personality. He was open to ideas, he was interested in my accent, where I came from, what was it like there? (And slightly sadly, what 'the pussy' was like . . . ?) Oh well, you can't have everything (as Paul Merton once said, 'Where would you keep it all?'), but I still think this kid's heart was in the right place. He must've been no more than seventeen. I hope the world leaves him alone and he has a few more dreams. Flowers don't often grow through the blacktop.

So Memphis: Well obviously, I'd like to investigate Elvis world, but the schedule is written, and I am just a passenger tonight, so we ship out at 2.40AM. I think I've had a couple of hours sleep somewhere. I won't see any more today, though. My arse/base of spine is really starting to hurt now. I've got a couple of positions I can move into, but none last for more than an hour, which makes sleep impossible.

The long faced, beardy chap plonks himself down next to me, and we talk a little bit, but it feels like we should try and kip in this darkness, so neither of us succeed to any great level, but we both try. Two and a half hours later, we're turfed out of the bus at Little Rock (AR) for a fifteen minute layover, so they can wash the bus and make sure we don't get too much sleep. Obviously, I smoke again. What else can you do in fifteen minutes?

At around 5.20AM, we pull out and continue on our way. Never stopping for long, never standing still; this journey carves its way through the days and across the landscape like an inevitable storm cloud scudding in the sky.

Ford Mustangs noted along with Harleys, truck drivers nodded to (eyes met and he raises one finger from the wheel with a smirk. Nice. I can't help myself smiling back at him, because of that, though), the landscape varies from plains to forests, hills to urban sprawls. This country rarely surprises you, but it does something vastly more important—it reassures you. All those films, all those songs—here they are before your very eyes; it was all true. Now you're in the middle of it; it's like you're in a film, and although you don't know the script, you know that someone's written one, because this film just keeps going.

. . . and if those films were all true, then generally, it's gonna be okay, yeah? The good guy always wins. And if this turns out to be a load of shit anyway, who really cares? What are you gonna do anyway?

Amarillo (TX). Oh yeah, I do know the way to bloody Amarillo, thanks (problem is, I wish I didn't). It was another cleaning stop, but this time we're here for an hour and fifteen, from nearly 5PM until gone six in the boiling heat.

I smoke a few cigarettes outside with some Mexicans. The white people are hiding in the shade, while the Mexicans sit in the sun. The social etiquette is to look down on these people if you're white, but I'm not from here, or likely to conform to that social convention, so I wander over and stand beside them. One in particular sees me rolling my own, and we start talking. He's got a large clear bag of rolling tobacco that he shows me, before rolling one from his stash. He's the only other person that I've seen smoking roll ups since I've been here, and we fall into easy conversation. He's been unemployed and homeless in LA and is now heading back to his ex-wife and kid, hoping to make amends and look for a better life. He doesn't seem to notice my accent, but I'm very conscious of the quick, sideways looks his fellow Mexicans give us as we chat about life and the economy. I wish him good luck as we part company to catch different buses.

'We could all do with some of that,' he replies with a warm smile.

Everyone seems relaxed around this journey, regardless of the shit they've been through.

I go inside the bus station, find the café, and order a black coffee.

'Oh honey, our coffee's not black, it's brown,' says the little old lady behind the counter, with a gentle southern drawl.

'Okay then, make it as brown as you can, without using any milk, please,' I reply and make her laugh.

I felt confident enough to be surrounded by black men and say this out loud. I'm sick of all that 'you can't say black' shit. Look, it's just coffee, it isn't any other bloody colour (unless you put other things in it, and I want mine with water and that's all). So please, keep that crap to yourself, eh?

Later, I ordered another and she said:

'Oh, is that your second?'

'Yeah, I had one early.'

'Well, it's only 25¢ for a fill up then.'

This was going well. I remembered her name (Charlotte) from the till receipt from the first coffee and thanked her, using it. She must've been in her mid to late fifties, and with a little banter going around the bus station café, we all contributed.

Eventually we had to ship out, and she asked me about myself, 'I just love your accent; where ya'll from?'

Texans aren't exactly cosmopolitan, but they are damned friendly and polite. We chatted for a while as I looked at some postcards, and she told me my accent reminded her of Piers Morgan. With mock horror on my face, I scolded her for saying such a thing, and we laughed out loud. Time was pressing, though, and I had to bid farewell, even though I'd have happily stayed a while longer in this lovely lady's café. Her smile and temperament had brightened my day no end.

Later in the journey, as Neil (the long faced, hippie-type, Grateful Deadhead, remember him from earlier?) and I sat on the floor in a McDonalds car park smoking and talking with the sunshine burning our brains, he said:

'I don't normally bother with conversations on Greyhounds, cause they (indicating the bus passengers) are not really worth it. There's nothing there (he indicates the brain), but you're different. It's been great talking with you, man. You're okay.'

His dad moved cars around the country on a transporter, and Neil ran a restaurant in Oklahoma. Now, at thirty-four, he was still a fresh, open mind. We had a lot in common mentally, sharing our opinions on almost every subject that either of us brought up to test the other. It was an amazing conversation, like we'd known each other for years and would for many more to come. There was a bond between us, and I was slightly annoyed when we had to get back on the bus. (He was at the back of the bus for some reason, being wound up by two brain dead young girls, apparently.) Neil was getting off next stop, but he suddenly came up to my seat as he was leaving the bus and placed a large, clear zippy bag in my hand containing about five Penguin biscuits worth of grass in it. Certainly more than I had ever seen.

'It's grass,' he whispered to me, quite loud enough for most of the people sitting around me to hear, '... I forgot I had it. Don't worry; I've got loads more vacuum sealed.'

And with a warm smile and a raised hand, he was gone.

In this final gesture, he had proved me right in my opinion of him and shown me another form of kindness. I had mentioned to him how I'd like to try a little Californian grass when I got there, meaning a joint or two. I had now been presented with enough free weed that I could consider a career change into drugs dealing or at the very least, never need to buy any ever again. This was ridiculous—in a country where the police regularly shoot the people that everyone else isn't shooting and drug dealing is still considered a social faux pas, I now had, about my person, a hell of a lot of 'strong grass,' as Neil pre-warned me before we parted at the bus station in Oklahoma.

I wish we'd swapped some more details or something, but maybe life is meant to be this way. I stashed the weed at the top of my only bag and had a cigarette, staring up at the royal blue skies and red brick buildings decaying around the bus station. It was a funny old world.

And the movie cameras continued to roll . . .

Of course, I was a sort of drugs trafficker now, as it was in my possession as I moved on the coach across the country. 'Wasn't this strictly illegal?' I wondered to myself. I seem to remember something involving Howard Marks. But as I hadn't bought it and didn't actually know it was drugs, having not tried it (smelt sure like weed to me, though!), and I didn't intend selling it—was I actually doing anything wrong?

Well, clearly, yes is the answer.

I looked at the massive lumps in the plastic bag and wondered what to do. I could just chuck it, Neil would never know, and I didn't want to hurt his feelings, after all, but then I'd said I wanted to try some, so it was my own fault. Part of me just liked the serendipity of the situation. I hadn't even got to California, and already I had more grass than I could ever smoke, even if I lived to be a hundred and fifty. On the other hand, I didn't want a long prison term to end this tale, though. It'd certainly be a spectacular finale, but then again, perhaps not.

I came up with a plan: I was going to see Greg Proops recording a comedy podcast in LA on the first night I was in town. He's always talking about how much he smokes it—I'll hand it to him as a present and instantly become his best pal. He would then take me under his wing and show me the celebrity lifestyle that he obviously leads and introduce me to television bosses and stars. It would only be a matter of time before I was starring in my own Hollywood blockbuster!

Well that was that. One more thing—I'd photograph the stash, because nobody would believe me about this back home. It was all too weird. My journey across the States was turning up some strange carpets in strange houses, and the dust was getting everywhere. So now I was 'carrying,' as they say. Luckily, I was a six foot, four inch tall, white male without any luggage, with a biker's leather jacket, long hair, and possibly the most English accent this side of Hackney. I blended in with everyone else like a blood stain on a wedding dress. Lucky I didn't actually smoke any of Neil's parting gift at this point, or I might've got a little paranoid . . .

Strangely, it didn't seem to worry me; I wasn't at all bothered. I knew what the possible outcomes could be, but I sort of knew that I would come to no harm too, as my plan was reasonable. I felt serene, as if I was floating through reality like a feather on the surface of a slow moving river. In retrospect, I might've been suffering from malnutrition, but it's hard to tell. Talk about hiding in plain sight.

Top tip time: if you're ever planning on smuggling drugs—as much as you might think your idea is fool proof (it isn't), don't shove them up an elephant's bum and expect to get through customs without so much as a whiff of pachyderm poo at the port of Dover.

However, an air of inevitability seemed to wash over me, as if someone had written this script and I was merely acting out a role within a much larger screenplay. I didn't even shove the stuff into my possessions—I placed the grass at the very top. If you opened the bag, you had to see it. I was laying down a challenge to the gods. Come on you bastards—prove you exist. I'm giving it to you on a plate! They weren't done with me yet, but like the fly fishermen that they are, playing the line is just the start of catching the fish. I was still able to make a choice about dumping the dope before I got to Phoenix (AZ) (incidentally, in completely unconnected news— also the name I chose for my last ever childhood soap box racer). The plan was solid, and I was my own mule.

Wednesday 30th May 2012

PHOENIX (AZ)
[ARSEHOLE ZOO]

LOS ANGELES (CA)
[CHRONIC ACTORS]

We hit Phoenix at 7AM. Well we were due to, but the night had brought some interesting developments. Some backseat shenanigans had occurred. Some drinking and abusive language had caused the words *Crips and Bloods* to be mentioned, and the next thing you knew, security guards were all over us as we pulled in for a layover. At this change station (Albuquerque, NM), the new bus driver (Kim) was harsh and decisive, instantly banning the kid with the motor mouth.

'You're not getting on my bus, kid,' she informed the angry youth.

She was also late.

So we were now late.

If it had been possible to wheel spin a Greyhound bus at 2AM on the empty streets of Albuquerque, then she probably got the closest. Her comfort stops were lightening affairs. And she retained her anger for the entire eight-hour journey. It was lucky she smoked too, or I'd swear she was trying to have a go at us anti-social types. I tried to break the ice with her using my amazing English accent but to no avail. She was almost as angry as the kid she'd chucked off.

She'd bark, 'Ten minutes, max' into the microphone, skid to a halt, jump out, and then be away before I was halfway down my cigarette.

Also for the first time in the journey, I saw her drive off and leave a passenger at a gas station at the end of a comfort stop in the middle of the night. This was an old lady, who had appeared to be a bit confused about what was happening. This was a bit harsh, but she was trying to reach our connections at other bus stations further down the line, so for some people on the bus, she must've been a bit of a star. I didn't think I liked her much.

While we waited for Angry Kim to turn up at the Albuquerque bus station, a small, tattooed blonde girl from the back of the bus clocked my Ramones T-shirt and started, when she heard the accent, 'Oh. You're British. Say cheerio,' she begged, to which, like an acquiescent monkey, I did. Much to her delight, I can report to you all. Oh look, a silly English fellow fulfilling a stereotype for an American idiot in a bus terminal. She looked a bit punky, but was with other white tattooed types, who certainly weren't interested in making a new pal.

'Say, what a bleddy mess, go on, say, what a bleddy mess!'

Although, I did get her back later with a 'shut it, you slaaag' that no-one else heard. I'm not sure she got the irony in the statement, but then I didn't expect her to.

Amongst the conversations that I overheard, I seemed to be the only married person on this journey. Everyone else had divorce or death (in one case) as part of their personal history.

The death was an old fellow (white moustache, tall, baseball cap, looked a bit like Sam Elliott) who'd been with us a while. He and I eventually spoke at one rest stop, and it turned out he'd worked for Goodyear tyres for twenty years, then his wife died, and now he spends his retirement travelling the buses and prospecting for gold. That's correct; he was a real gold digger! He worked a ten-hour day, five for the company digging for gold, then he was allowed to dig another five hours for himself. Anything he found in his five hours was his to keep. And not only that, whatever the company had made at the end of the month, there was a bonus shared between those that had dug. Regularly, he'd get $10K as his share, due to the price of gold going mad recently. It was, therefore, less of a surprise when he said he'd just lost $16K in a casino in twelve hours partying with his daughter. He didn't look unhappy in the slightest.

We ploughed across the desert landscape, exactly as you know in your mind when you think of 'cowboy movie.' All those three-pronged cacti everywhere, little flat pancake ones with spines—it was all there ticking those eye spy book boxes of my childhood. I even saw, and I swear on my life it's true, actual, real, tumbleweed! This stuff was green, but it was the real thing, without a doubt.

Oh, and a little tornado or two in the Arizona (AZ) desert as the wind picked up the dust ahead of us and lorries (sorry, 'trucks') pulled over to the side of the road, rather than being tipped in mid-gear change. They weren't frightening to me in my heightened state of serene fantasy, but the middle aged Mexican woman now sitting next to me could hardly stand it. Her reactions of shock were a silent movie to my iPod that was playing a comedy podcast. I tried not to laugh out loud, but I can't swear nobody heard me. It probably reinforced what they thought about the stiff upper lipped British laughing in the face of death. Let's hope so. It could so easily have appeared that I thought the fear of an older woman to be something humorous. And that's not going to go down well anywhere this side of Afghanistan, even if there is a spark of truth in it.

We were buffeted by the twister as we crawled across the open expanse following the only choice of road available, passing the trucks that had pulled in. Obviously, our newest driver was either foolhardy or braver than the legendary American trucker.

He thought I sounded like Piers Morgan when we chatted later. He meant it in a nice way, he said when I acted horrified. This was becoming ridiculous. He was an old man who had a Memphis southern drawl—slow and low, which felt like honey dripping in your ears when he spoke.

Unlike most drivers, he was something beyond his job. He spoke like an old hand, unworried, unstressed, and without the need to express authority just because he had it. Quiet jokes filled the air in lazy sunshine of the afternoon. Without any introduction, out of nowhere, he started telling us all a story, as he drove us away from a comfort stop, in his warm drawl.

'Back there at that last stop there used to be an Indian fellow working. He doesn't work there anymore. One day he did one of those scratch cards, the sevens one, I think, and anyway, he gets the jackpot. I used to know him, you know? But he's gone now. Anyway, he takes the card to a different place to claim it, cos he doesn't want them to think there's anything underhand going on, and so they go upstairs to check it, leaving him down in the shop. This goes on for a while, about half an hour he's waiting there, so he plays a few more cards, and would you believe it, he wins again on their cards. Not as much as the first time … but still.'

The driver pauses for a few dramatic seconds and then asks the bus, 'How much d'ya reckon he won in total then?'

People start shouting out life-changing amounts, starting at a million dollars and going upwards, but eventually the driver comes back on the microphone and gives us the actual answer, 'Two hundred and seven thousand dollars,' and finishes the tale with a resigned aside, 'Lucky fella.'

It's not as much as we'd expected, but even in the disappointment, we're all wishing we were in his boots right now. These seats were really starting to take their toll.

When we finally parted with this old driver, I hung around until everyone else had got off the bus and made a point of talking to him, which he seemed happy to do. I said how much pleasure I had by listening to him throughout our eight hours together on the bus, which seemed to genuinely please him. Then he started talking about bees.

'Have you heard about the fella, Brother Adam at Buckfastleigh, the priest? Well I had some of his bees. Had me seven hives making some fine honey.'

This was a rare and kindly man, and I wished I'd been able to know him more than just our time together on the Greyhound. Regret is the brother to travel.

Now; back to our newest and angriest driver, Kim. We tanked across the deserts and down the highest, steepest hills of the journey so far, ending up in Phoenix (AZ) by about 8AM. We were late getting in but still easily in time, as the bus wasn't due out before 8.30AM. Unfortunately, nobody got on it, because we were all told to stand in a queue in the Phoenix bus station and told our bus would be there in a minute. It was just being washed or something.

Kim was applauded by one particularly noisy black girl from downtown LA (I'll call her Jade, although that wasn't her name). Hollering, whooping, and clapping like a demented cheerleader, Jade kept up a running commentary that needed no microphone.

There were a few like her on the bus journey—those that were more than fond of their own voices. Volume was their status. Why they thought we gave a rat's arse what they thought about anything is beyond me. Perhaps it was just a nervous tick kind of thing, where they had to say something in case they just disappeared. Whatever the cause, they just couldn't shut up.

So there was some kind of karma thing going on when, as we stood in the bus station in Phoenix, somebody nicked Jade's cell phone from a free charging port. Talk about a captive audience. She hollered, she screamed abuse at the mystery thief, she cursed their family, she abused the security bloke and other members of the Greyhound staff. Stalking the bus station, complete strangers from other buses got a performance of toys being thrown out of the pram at such an echoing volume you'd have thought at least one person would've just turned around and smacked her at some point. But nobody did. I'm surprised nobody shot her. They just stood and watched the insanity. She couldn't ring her phone, because it had been turned off at the charging dock that was helpfully supplied free to its customers by Greyhound Inc. I spoke more with the blonde punk girl.

'I married a Russian bloke once.'

She then said something in Russian to me, which I (obviously) didn't understand or, being the social dead end that I am, didn't choose to bother asking her to translate. She looked disappointed that I wasn't impressed and pushed on with her theme:

'Look, here's a Russian tattoo I had done.'

Her right arm revealed a hammer and sickle amongst a sleeve of coloured images. I smiled at her in either an impressed or blank way, depending from which side you viewed it. One of my few skills is having a blank face and showing an almost sullen lack of interest when I should be smiling or acknowledging people. I've been told it looks quite rude. I'm inwardly quite proud about this (but I try not to show it). My apathy finally began to sink in, and she drifted away.

It appears we are going to be late, and our bus is not coming. We were meant to leave this white, echoing cement block by 8.25AM, but now they're saying it'll be 11.50AM, and then things get vague and we finally realise we are screwed, as all hope trickles away.

I wander outside to the rear of the building, where a car park holds a few taxis and vast amount of over-heated air. I make my way slowly over to a taxi parked in the shade of some palm trees and ask the driver how much it'd cost to take me to LA.

'Where in LA?' (suspiciously)

'The Hollywood Hills. West Hollywood?'

'Where is that?' (he looks confused, which is understandable, considering I've just told him the location and he is a person who's entire profession is based on locations of places).

'LA'

'How far is it?' (This is promising; he's clearly aware that it isn't here.)

'I don't know; I thought you might know.'

'And you want a taxi there?' (You can't say he doesn't catch on quickly, this one.)

'Yeah.'

'How much are you looking at spending?' (A good question, but I'm worried his mathematical skills may be on a par with his other, spatial awareness skills, and we may find ourselves in uncharted territory soon.)

'As little as possible.'

He pauses and looks quizzically at me.

'Give me a number' (misquoting Johnny Ball and tempting me to go all existential on his ass).

But I rein myself in. I know how to haggle.

'No. You give me your figure, and we'll work down from there.'

His fellow cabbies are smirking now at our conversation; they clearly like to see this bossy bloke being given the run around.

'Where is it?' (He's not giving me much faith in his ability to locate places with this display of early onset dementia.)

'About forty dollars north of the downtown Greyhound bus station,' I say, mixing finance with distance to show that he can't out-obtuse me.

All the while we've been talking, he's been looking at and pressing the buttons on a satnav trying to find the distance. Finally, the prize is his:

'That's over four hundred miles away!'

(Now we know.)

'Okay. So?'

'How much are you thinking of paying?' (Ahh, that old chestnut. Haven't we been here before?)

'Less than you want,' I reply (more sniggers from the fellow cabbies).

'Somewhere between seven hundred and nine hundred dollars then,' concludes the hapless cabbie after a long ponder.

He looks hopefully up from his calculations, like a child waiting for praise from his parent. 'Oh,' I pause, 'Okay. Well, that's not even in the ball park then. Okay. No need to even haggle here,' I conclude. And as his little face falls, I turn to go back to the bus station, but he stops me with a call.

'How much would you be thinking of?' (Those slippery straws can be a bugger to hold, can't they?)

'No more than two hundred and fifty dollars,' I replied casually.

'That wouldn't even cover the cost of the fuel,' his shock is almost palpable (and they say fuel is cheap out here).

'That's okay. No bother.' I turn away once more, but he calls me back again and writes out a card with his phone number on it, handing it to me with a hopeful smile.

'Have a think about it. Give me a call if you change your mind.'

'Thanks.' I pocket the card, and as I walk into the coolness of the station, stick it on top of a coke machine.

Then I hear the rumour that's now going around; that it'll be nearer 1.30PM when we get to leave this place.

I hate Phoenix.

Inside, Jade is still hollering, and almost as loudly, I hear the Tannoy say something about all passengers agreeing to allow all baggage to be searched for the missing phone. Oh yeah, I forgot.

I'm still carrying that massive wedge of dope, aren't I?

The piggy security guard has white latex gloves on at all times, as if he's expecting a rushed demand for a quick internal examination. I try not to catch his eye. But like I said before, I do stick out a bit. His station is at the end of our queue, and I try not to look nervous. I smoke outside and know that if Jade doesn't shut the fuck up, we might all get our belongings searched. It was bad enough being told we'd have to stay here under the watchful eye of Piggy Malone, but she's really not helping. Now it might be even longer? Now those taxi prices were beginning to look more reasonable, if I could just get two others to share. But look at this bloody shower—they wouldn't split a banana, let alone a taxi fare with me. Oh shut up, Jade, for fuck sake, shut up!

I couldn't leave my bag or claim it wasn't mine. It had my passport in it. I sat down and angrily pulled out my iPod and played some music to myself and a game of backgammon (which I won) (obviously). Neil had mentioned that the airports had dogs, and sometimes the bus stations did too. Phoenix didn't appear to be canine compatible at the moment, but would they suddenly appear, now I was side by side with my bag? I got up for another cigarette and found my tobacco was running low. Things were becoming desperate. Slowly I had become oblivious to the posturing of the blacks around me. I looked more random than they could ever be, and I felt they instinctively looked away when I looked towards them. I was not of them, and now they knew it.

I stepped back into the vast bus station, necked a $3.75 bottle of cold water, and returned to my smoking.

Suddenly Jade has shut up. Oh, Jade has found her phone. One girl looked at me as we smoked.

'I'm glad she found it, I don't think I could've stood that for another seven hours!'

Although I knew what she meant, I wondered if that was a confession at the same time, because she went on to tell me that the phone had been found out here on the smoker's bench apparently, where the thief had been scared into leaving it. She stubbed out her cigarette and went inside.

Eventually, a bus turned up for us at 11.50AM, and we filed on board like the sheep we were. Bus tickets ruthlessly checked for the first time since New York for some reason, under the watchful eyes of Piggy and his white gloves. Was this because of it ending in LA? I've never been so paranoid, and yet at the same time, I felt supremely calm.

The survivors from the original bus got onto our final coach to LA. Here we all were once more; another female driver, another seat, all ready to pull away for our final road trip. Then suddenly a load of other people started to file onto the coach. We were more packed in than at any other part of the journey. Greyhound had combined two coachloads into one bus, and now our motley gang were surrounded by interlopers. This was ridiculous. We were due in LA at 3.45PM (originally); now we'd be lucky if we made it by 7PM. At which point, I then had to get a taxi to the home in the hills, wash and shower (after three days on the road), and get back out to Bar Lubitsch on Santa Monica Boulevard to see Greg and offload some of this stash.

So we're going for a bit, and then we pull in for a comfort stop at the back of a filling station somewhere in the Nevada desert.

It feels like 1,000 degrees out here in the sun as I have a couple of smokes. I stay close to the bus; I don't want to be one of the ones left behind. Next thing I see is two cops getting on our bus. Oh, for fuck sake! I point out the police to a big black woman standing nearby having a smoke.

'Oh yeah, they put ex-felons on Greyhounds just outside California.'

They do this, apparently, so that the recently released criminals can look all normal when they get into LA and get off a standard bus, so they can start afresh, without the visual stigma of being an ex-felon. (How nice for them.)

Now part of me is relieved they don't have sniffer dogs with them and part of me thinks,

'What did this ex-felon do to become one, and are we now in danger of becoming another newspaper headline?'

The police wander up the bus with their charge, straight past my seat (where the block of weed sits waiting in my bag), right to the back of the bus and then back out again. Two sweeps and no alarm bells.

So we may have another killer amongst us, this time with a little proof to his claims. Lucky we weren't already packed in like bloody sweaty sardines. Three squad cars and a secure prison pickup/van combo pull away into the dust. This just gets weirder and weirder.

Next, there is some sort of border check point at California. I don't know why; every other state has just been happy with a street sign telling us where we were. California wants to talk to our bus driver, have a quick squint at her passengers, and get some paperwork signed for some reason. It's almost as if we were entering a whole new country. There was clearly a police dog van parked amongst the security cars around the checkpoint. I hope they had the window down (but not too far). Finally, they allow us to enter California, and we sweep down the long, flat empty highway. Straight two lane road slicing the country up. There's nothing to look at; it's like driving across the moon; even the horizon has no features. To be honest, the first four hours in the Californian sun is so deeply boring I keep expecting to see the boys from Journey hitchhiking. It is an alien landscape out there; rocks, scrubby plants, and a few volcanic hillsides.

Jade is upfront broadcasting Bullshit FM to all who haven't put their ear plugs in. I'm too close for even that to work, so I turn on the iPod and relieve it for a while. The traffic starts to build up around us, but the straight roads just seem to go on forever, without so much as a house or filling station to break the monotony.

A Mexican lad shows me some respect as I struggle from my seat to follow the fat Mexican truck driver, who has been sitting next to me, out of the coach into the insane heat of California. We light up, acknowledging each other like the new loose gang that we have become. Generally, it seems that the Mexicans have much more respect (or good manners, if you will) than the black kids or the tattooed whites. I feel more at home with them and want to talk to the Mexican truck driver. He is, like quite a few on the trip, a driver going to pick up a rig somewhere else. They don't seem to own their own or work for a company with a regular ride. He tells me California imposes its own rules about fuel and that they charge a tax on everyone who goes there. He has to have four fuel tanks on his rig because of them; the normal three and a fourth one with cleaner fuel the Californians will accept. Which means he's got to stretch his supply as he crosses the border or get fined. I tell him about how we all had to put additives in our fuel when the four-star petrol changed to unleaded after he says the car drivers have to use an additive in their fuel for the same reasons.

I think the Mexicans are looked down upon by everyone in the US, and so, when I treat them just like anyone else, they really appreciate it and respond. Us Brits always like the underdogs, don't we? I noticed the sideways looks I got from the blacks and whites when they saw me chatting casually with the Mexicans. And I didn't mind that one bit. The Mexicans smiled when we spoke and offered to share their food. They were quiet people; proud, but clearly struggling.

So more and more miles rolled under our wheels as we bounced along over every pothole created in the history of road travel. After three and a half days of this, my arse was so painful. It was basically the base of my spine that was taking a pounding. The top of your arse (not to be used as a greeting in Ireland, if you want to keep on the outside of your pint) is just where your two buttocks separate and become your lower back. At this crucial point, I was trying to suspend my body weight and even tried holding myself up with my hands rather than be forced to lower myself upon the seat—bus yoga.

The desert landscape slowly took us into the legendary Joshua Tree National Park, although from the road the actual trees were hard to see. I looked hard to see if Bono was wandering around raising Cain or the burning corpse of Gram Parsons was still smouldering nearby, but alas, no. (Probably another example of health and safety gone mad.) The road we were riding was straight as an arrow that wasn't bent; two parallel lanes heading into Los Angeles and two heading straight out. Across the flat lunar tundra, (yeah, I've thought twice about using that word here, but I've decided to leave it in anyway. *Tundra*. Let's see if it annoys us), we headed for the horizon, which eventually rose out of the flatness and appeared to be a mountain range.

What it actually was, was the barrier between nature and the jolly seaside resort of absolute lunacy. As we finally reached this rocky outcrop and the roads carved through it, we finally started the decent into the city where nearly eighteen million Americans call home (and everyone else calls 'La La Land'). They had a surprise for those brave enough to venture into the city via the desert road. Before you got to Los Angeles the very edge of the desert is a massive wind farm. Four thousand, eight hundred giant windmills of various sizes turn constantly at the Gorgonio Pass, creating electricity for the city beyond the ridge. It took a good half an hour to drive past them at 60mph. Breath taking is how America likes to surprise you, and here was another example. No sign of Windy Miller's cousin, Randy, though.

The closer we got to the Los Angeles bus station, the further away it seemed to get. We'd stop somewhere, someone would get off, and when we re-joined the freeway it would say something like 150 miles to Los Angeles every time. It never seemed to get any closer, and we kept making these silly little stops where just the one person would get off or one would get on. In a road journey of three and a half thousand miles, we must've made more stops in the last eight hours in California than we did in the rest combined. It was truly unbelievable.

The evening traffic was mainly leaving the city on the (now) six lanes in either direction. The view from the window was all squalor as we swooped down into suburbia; rusty old cars, broken down and boarded houses, nobody on the streets. Abandoned traces of previous lives.

We pulled in to a station, and I thought my chance had come, but alas, it was just another false alarm. A few got off, and on we trundled with twelve lanes of traffic, mainly cars buzzing past us and cutting in, but with little or no indication of their intent. It wasn't surprising that there were no bikers around. I imagine most had been run down early on by these madmen around us.

Crawling along through increasingly smoggy and industrial lined freeways, stopping occasionally to deposit the odd person in some dead end side street, it seemed that time began to stretch out before us like a rubber band. Ever so slowly we inched our way forward as the hours ticked away. Having entered the city of Los Angeles two hours ago, we seemed to be no nearer to the end than when we started.

And then suddenly, in the evening sunshine, we pulled into Los Angeles city bus station, our final destination. As the dusty old bus turned into the empty car park, I spied a couple of yellow cabs loitering behind a wall. That had been my biggest worry actually; the chance of not getting a taxi to my home in the hills where I needed to drop my stuff off into and then equally quickly leg it down to see Greg on Santa Monica Boulevard, offload some of my dope, and become a free agent once again. A lot of the bus stations along the way hadn't had any cabs outside when we pulled up in the past, and as the guidebook had said that you couldn't just hail one like you do in New York (or London), I had feared the worst. Time was running out. It was 7.30PM.

I turned to my fellow travellers on the steps of the bus as we trooped out,

'Hey guys—this has all been so much fun! Let's make it an annual get together, shall we?' And then, without waiting for a reply, I sprinted around the corner for the yellow cab.

Only Jade had the grace to acknowledge my shout with a not surprising,

'No fucking way!'

I think most of us promised ourselves never to travel by Greyhound again at this point, but I honestly believe most of them will. I may even myself, when the physical pain becomes a vague memory.

I jumped into the yellow cab and gave my driver, an old deaf Latvian (this is a market cornered, '80s American sitcom, fans!) the directions for my home in the hills. We bargained out a deal as the car rolled smoothly away from the Greyhound. He was to wait for me at my place, then drive me down to the Bar Lubitsch, and finally, to pick me up again at midnight.

It was fabulous to be free of the coach restraints after three and a half days. Comfortable seats, oh how I'd missed you! Seatbelts— only the driver on the Greyhound got that safety feature, an accelerator that goes higher than a slow crawl, and suspension that could deal with things lumpier than custard. Oh yes, goodbye Greyhound, goodbye!

Using the ubiquitous satnav, Sam (my driver) found the house easily enough (2797 Creston Drive). No-one was home. But the gate was unlocked and so was the door to my little private room (as seen in the photos online at AIRBNB. This was my first time ever using the service, and it was exactly as it had said online. Cool), so I slung my bag on the floor, rushed into the bathroom, and washed my hair. I was going to have a shower, but time was against me now. I took a lump off the block of grass and stuffed what amounted to a paperback books worth into my pocket. I was back out to the cab in ten minutes, having written a note for my host, Jackie, explaining what had happened. I stuffed it in their door frame, as there was no letter box. I saw through the window that there were two little dogs watching telly alone, and then they barked at me, but no-one human was home, so I dived back into the car, and we were off again. I paid over the price to Sam, with the promise from him of a return pick up at midnight, and ran into the club.

At the bar (a dingy little hole with a dingier back room scattered with cheap chairs), Greg was already mid-set, and so I tried to quickly get into the atmosphere. It was dark in the audience, and figures brushed past you as they looked for tables. I of course, stood at the back, glad to not be sitting down for once. Generally there isn't any audience interaction with these podcasts, because Greg is sharing his thoughts and is only after the occasional laugh, but I did get a laugh near the end of the recording, by shouting out 'Execute!' when Greg was struggling for an 'ex' word to describe what should happen to the senators. It was pretty quick of me I thought, as the

'Richard Hammond' character from the US version of *Top Gear* ducked down below me with his stunning (and significantly taller) girlfriend. I'd no idea who he was until afterwards when I was talking to Greg and so was he. I'd quite liked him up until I found out who he was (I eavesdropped his conversation and thought how vacant and 'showbiz' he seemed to be).

[To this day, you can still hear me shout out 'Execute!' on the podcast. (It's called 'The Smartest Man In The World' podcast, by the way. The episode in question is called 'Summers' and it's dated the 8th June, due to post-editing. It's easy enough to find on iTunes; other providers are probably available. But who gives a shit about them?)]

When my turn came, we shook hands, and I stuffed the weed into his outside pocket (which was the only pocket that could accommodate it in Greg's jacket).

'I think you'll like this, Greg,' I said with a smile.

He raised his eyebrows and smiled with a polite, 'Well, thank you.'

Greg was as gracious as you'd expect and startled when I said I'd travelled from Cornwall in the UK to see him tonight. I did the usual fan boy stuff, and then he was away into the night. Didn't get to buy him a drink, which was a shame. Saw his wife, though— very nice looking. It's funny, actually, how American Hammond's girlfriend and Greg's wife seemed to get very little attention; almost a little sexist, I'd say. But it's all entertainment bollocks really—a façade without depth, so not to worry.

A teenage starlet petitioned Greg as he left the venue. She was full of enthusiasm to tell him how women should rule the world. He was gracious again, probably due to her pneumatic nature, but let's not paint this too richly. I listened in and even I wanted to give her a smack (may be I'd been on the Greyhound for too long). When he'd left, the rest of the kids turned up to watch some truly bad stand-up comedy. They hadn't come to see a professional do it for free, but they'd turn up to support their lame mates for ten dollars; utter fools, the lot of them.

The women were, as famously advertised, fantastically beautiful, and (also as famously advertised) fantastically vacant. I stood outside and talked to Connor, the doorman. He was, after me, probably the next oldest person in the bar, at nearly thirty years old. He was working as the doorman this particular night, but he often worked behind the bar. He told me how he'd soon be married after an eight year courtship, and he turned out to be another cool chap who seemed to be genuinely interesting. We spoke for a long time about life in general, kids, etc. But time was pushing on, and eventually Sam picked me up in his yellow cab and whisked me, once again, up the hill to my resting place.

The house was quiet, my note was gone, and so I crawled into my bed and slept horizontally for the first time in four nights. I wonder if Greg slept as well as I did?

[It says 1966–the year I was born, trivia fans.]

Thursday 31st May 2012

LOS ANGELES . . .

My first morning in the Hollywood Hills: As I walked out of my door, a bloke with a large bag was coming down some stairs by the house. He didn't seem very talkative or happy to see me, so I assumed he wasn't the owner, Corey (whom I hadn't actually seen a picture of yet). I knocked on the door where I'd left the note the night before, and it was opened by a bearded bloke in shorts. This was Corey. He said goodbye to 'Eric' as he passed through the back gate and invited me into the main house for a coffee and a chat. Then he took me around the garden and up to the water tank to show me the views. It was breathtaking. There was a fantastic view over LA on one side and possibly an even better view of the lake (reservoir) on the other.

It was so contrasting; one side the hub of human relentlessness, and the other, nature in full attack (although the lake is man-made, it does look good).

He left me after a while, and I pattered around, ringing home to tell Ju I was okay. I left it a bit late in the day, but went down to a local supermarket at the bottom of the hill to get some food, when my phone went tits up and ran out of credit. It was so hot, and I was sweating like a dog by the time I got back. It must've been at least

32 degrees, and the hill was really, really steep (like one in two, in old money). I think I nearly died there for a minute.

After a shower (*thank god!*), I met Corey's partner, Jackie, and she gave me the *Ugly Things Magazine* that had come for me in their post. It was massive! More like a flipping book than a magazine, but the review was quite good, so I lay on a nearby sun lounger and read the paper, relaxed (as you do), and wondered how it all went so badly wrong between sips of my ice cold margarita.

The house clings to the side of the highest part of the hill, and work was being done to renovate rooms, so there were lots of Mexicans and noise, but nothing bothered me in the sunshine. The structure was a funny combination of modern glass walls and windows and old red brick surrounded by random patios and little steps. Corey told me that the house had been owned by the same owner from its start for about sixty odd years, and then someone else for twelve years, and now he had it. A lot of renovation needed to be done, as the previous owners hadn't put much effort into that area. It also allowed him to get more people to rent rooms from AIRBNB, the company I'd used to find him.

The Beatles had stayed down the road in the castle-like house that Moby now owned but had come up to the water tower to take acid apparently. I could imagine them doing just that, as I wandered around the curved steel walls. Apparently, they were there around the *Live at the Hollywood Bowl* album that was recorded in either August 1964 or August 1965. Coincidently, the paper I was reading said that The Beach Boys (with the full band for the first time in a zillion years, including Brian) were playing in the Hollywood Bowl tomorrow. It's only on the other side of the hill surrounding the lake, and you can often hear it really well, so I was told by Corey.

The day rolled into night, and I slept easy until the early morning, when three different rubbish trucks picked up right outside my bedroom window. Oh, so there are some bad points about this then? Okay, well just the odd niggle here and there, but let's not let it spoil such a magnificent journey. I decided to go back up to the water tank with my cigarettes, my iPod, and a bottle of Glenfiddich whisky. Life's a bummer sometimes, ain't it?

[The view looking back up the hill]

Los Angeles . . . Still

I tried to ring Julie back in Cornwall, 6,000 miles away. But the phone cut out, and then I realised my mobile credit was gone. This was in the days of PAYG, before common sense walked up to me and smacked me in the chops. I couldn't even text her now. I am such a plank.

Early in the day, I walked down to the supermarket again and then just kept walking. I was looking for a payphone and marvelling at the old cars rusting ever so slowly in the Californian sun along the road, checking out the houses in the dry heat, and beginning to get a feel for the way people lived here. Down on the flat, the houses were older and similar to each other, nothing insanely posh, but as you climbed the hill, you found every single house was different from its neighbour, and yet still, the clearly posh residents sat cheek by jowl next to more ramshackle creations. Old money holding on as new money squeezed in next door.

About two and a half miles away, I found a payphone that worked and tried to call Julie again. It was then that I realised I didn't have her mobile number on me.

Ffs!

I tried our home number, but obviously, they had gone by then. My card told me I was down to fifty minutes or so, but that didn't worry me. I left it a day and then walked all the way down to Franklin again on Sunday, the third, to call Julie's mobile. This time the card told me I only had eight minutes credit left now, and it wouldn't connect me to her phone anymore, anyway. I'll just have to call from New York City and hope she's not too worried about me. This is really annoying. Next time I'll find a way to use my mobile out here, regardless of cost (hindsight is a wonderful thing).

Saw a hummingbird in the wild, just outside Moby's house. A real, wild hummingbird. My mind was completely blown for the rest of the day. I didn't expect to ever see one of these tiny birds in the flesh, let alone in the wild. It buzzed up to me, hovered for a second, and then zipped away in a flash. A brilliant blue thing half the size of a crème egg.

Friday was spent working on the book. I mooched around after breakfast, and then the muse took me around 11AM and I worked for six hours straight, writing feverishly. Eventually drained, I relaxed with some whisky and peanuts, trying to watch a great film about Ernest Hemmingway called *Hemingway and Gellhorn*. Coincidently, the only book I brought with me to read was Hemingway's *A Movable Feast*, and so it seems that I've moved from Bukowski to Hem in my affections.

Six hours of writing longhand exhausts you, trying to get it all down, trying to make sense of it all, recalling quotes, making value judgements; images, sounds, and smells must all be in place before the memory fades and an air of falsehood descends. There's no real time to reflect on the journey at this stage, because I'm still only half way through it, but being as the first half will be so different from the second, a certain amount of conclusion can be drawn, albeit tainted by proximity.

As expected (by myself at least), the travellers on the Greyhound were the underclasses and uneducated. They were not unhappy or aggressive (particularly), but they were aware of their position in life and could still look down on the homeless and Mexicans, if nothing else. Most seemed to have some connection with crime, most appeared to be ethnic origin, and most seemed to be quite vocal. The age range was complete, from babes in arms to grandmothers and all in between. Gender-wise, again it was evenly split, with young men taking most of the male vote and older women taking most of the female side. Greyhound employee stats were as follows— bus drivers (sixty per cent men), ticket sales and advice at bus stations (one hundred per cent women), security (eighty per cent

*men), clerks/cleaners/station workers (one hundred per cent men)
and café staff (eighty per cent women). Of course, this is only my
experience over my journey; read into this what you will.*

[Some useful roadside information for the local lawbreaker]

Saturday 2nd June 2012

LOS ANGELES . . .
[NOT LONDON APPRENTICE]

Started on the book early and got a line on it, doing a straight four-hour stint through until after lunch. Then I relaxed for the rest of the day, listening to my iPod and finishing the whisky. Running low on food, I decided to go down tomorrow, when I would also try and phone Julie once more (see earlier).

If you're interested in a weather report, I have one for you; scorchio!

Cory's seventeen year old daughter from his first wife is staying over from Colorado, travelling in her nice, new posh Range Rover. (It's nice to have money, isn't it?) Cory seems to be involved in the music business somehow, judging from the odd gold disc lying around the place. He works in the dance music field, because, 'that's where the money is.' Jackie said something about writing lyrics the other day in passing, so perhaps she's in it too. I didn't think lyrics were that important in dance music, but then, what do I know? He reckons the extra rooms on the house will mean he doesn't have to pay for his own part of the building anymore, with all the money coming in from AIRBNB. I hope so; it's such a nice place, but as I said to him,

'I wouldn't want to share this place with anyone; I'd prefer having the privacy.'

Luckily for me and all the others (from amongst other places— Mongolia, apparently), Corey doesn't feel like this and wants to share his house.

I ended the day listening to comedy on the TV. The picture went all negative after a while, but you could still hear the stand up.

I didn't really feel like going down into Los Angeles and investigating the city much and had no reply from my so-called friend, Ian Webber, about meeting up with him, so I stayed put in the hills. It was nice to relax and not have any missions to complete, to let the days slip past and just enjoy the peace that surrounded me. It was always sunny; it was always warm, I had alcohol and cigarettes, music on my iPod, and a book to both read and write. It was wonderfully freeing to allow myself this break and just calm down after riding the dog without sleep for so long. My lower spine was completely numb, which was both worrying and pleasantly painless. Sleep was easy.

[Oh baby, come to daddy!]

Sunday 3rd June 2012

Los Angeles . . .
Bye Bye La La

Last full day and night here—tomorrow it's the Amtrak experience.

My back has been weird since the Greyhound. The base of my spine is still completely numb, like someone has given me an injection down there. The skin is numb. Now, I don't expect it's anything serious or permanent, but after three nights, I sort of expected it to return to normal. I am slightly concerned that some permanent damage to my spine has been done, but as it's not affecting anything else at the moment, I think I'll just wait and see what happens. Trying to keep it protected when I sit, just in case.

I walked down the hill to try and use the phone on Franklin early in the day, but to no avail, so on the way back I bought some groceries and postcards and generally just kicked back (after I'd released the Sherpas from their service helping me back up the mountain).

Beforehand, I chatted to the manager of the local supermarket, as he was the only one working and I needed him to unlock the Jack Daniels bottles for me. He was a very gentle soul, quietly spoken, gracious, and pleasant. It was a nice moment, after the disappointment of not being able to talk to Julie and the kids.

But by seven o'clock in the evening, I was sitting back in my room on my last night in Los Angeles.

It's a strange feeling, because having spent a great deal of my time here in Los Angeles writing, it's almost as if I've only just got here, and now I've got to go again. I'm looking forward to NYC obviously, but I wonder if I'll ever come back to LA? As it stands now, I don't see any great reason to. If I was ever this side again, I think I'd head for Frisco, as it sounds like a more artistic and less vacuous place.

STAGE THREE

THE IRON HORSE

Los Angeles (CA)
[Christ Almighty!]

Flagstaff (AZ)
[Anal Zebras]

Finding Johnny McDonald

Woke early (as expected) and decided to hit the hill first and watch LA wake up. Smokes, coffee, and some Byrds on the iPod as the early mist crawled up the hillside and cooled the brushwood at my feet. Corey had said that rattlers hung around up here, and although I always wore my boots and looked carefully, I never saw or heard a single one. Part of me was disappointed, part of me delighted. (I think it was my legs that were most delighted.) I drank the rapidly cooling coffee and smoked the remaining six or seven cigarettes from the red, paper pack of Marlboro. Took one last long gaze at the Mullholland Dam and then slowly trudged back to my room. I had bought myself a half-bottle of Jack Daniels the night before, but the neck was all I could drink, and so, along with unopened cola, peanuts, and onion bagels, I left the bottle for Jackie and Corey. It was really just a space issue, and I'd have loved to take the JD—such is life.

By about 9.30, I thought I'd better make a move, and after a last shower, I packed up and asked Corey to ring a taxi for me (I tried to explain about the lack of cell phone, but I don't think he understood really). I waited and chatted to the workers that had arrived to continue the building work. It didn't take long for my taxi to arrive, and with a final farewell to Corey, I was away to the Union Railway Station. The taxi driver thought I sounded Australian, so I put on a strong Aussie accent to illustrate how un-Australian I was and asked the old fella where he came from.

'The former Russian republic.'

'Oh yeah, whereabouts?'

'Russia'

Why didn't he just say that in the first place? What's with all the 'former' stuff? Anyhow, he was quick enough, and I was at the railway station by 10AM. Only another eight hours to go before my train leaves.

So what's a poor boy to do?

Well, I bought some postcards and a newspaper, had a coffee, and stood outside smoking cigarettes, fending off people begging and assorted weirdos. They home in on bus stations and railway stations for some reason. Airports is where the big money is—that's where I'd panhandle, mate! Look at all those high rollers with their 'club class,' their 'business class' and their 'up yours, poor person class'—they've got spare change coming out their asses, good buddy!

Anyhow, I'm minding my own business, eavesdropping all the black kids jive talking (that's young person's slang for colloquial chatter, possibly) (ahem), when a tall, thin, old bloke wearing a battered Panama hat and a dirty white suit sits down next to me and places his walking stick on the edge of the bench. He's dressed like Tom Wolfe's granddad and looks not dissimilar to Richard Harris on his off days.

'Alright old man? Mind if I sit here?' he asks as he turns to me, lighting a cigarette.

'Not at all.'

His voice is like the sound of somebody either a hundred years behind the cigarette or a person a day away from having his vocal chords removed due to overuse. He just about hisses the words out.

He introduces himself,

'My name's Alan Flora,' he pauses and then adds, 'from Indianapolis,' as if an afterthought had occurred to him.

He raises an eyebrow to match his relaxed smile,

'Where you from?'

And so my introduction to the amazing world of Alan Flora has begun.

He is extremely engaging, considering he's missed his train for two days in a row and has had his bag stolen. Alan is due to travel on the same train as me, and so we chat and smoke together until we get moved on to the 'official' smoking area by a black woman of vast proportions squeezed into an optimistic station uniform.

We make an incongruous pair; an old man in a battered white suit and Panama, stooping slightly with his walking stick and a much taller, younger man in a biker's jacket and dark sunglasses. A bloke with a large camera comes up to us. He asks if he can take our photos.

'Aww, take this fella's photo, he's from England,' says Alan.

'He's English,' he adds, almost conspiratorially to the photographer, and he pulls me to him.

I pull away.

'Alan, it's you he's interested in, mate. You've got a lived-in face. Mine's just youthful and ugly.'

And I'm right, as it turns out; he doesn't want to photograph me. Alan, looking more like a bum than ever, poses for the camera with his cane. Like an old ham from vaudeville, he tips his hat to the photographer and throws wild shapes with his arms. The photographer asks Alan about his life as he snaps away, asking where he comes from and why he's here. It turns out Mr. Snappy is apparently working on a 'project called fifty people from fifty states' (that's why he's not interested in me), and he's loving Alan's wild theatrical gestures, but soon it's all over and we are alone once more.

'Hey, English, let's go and sit down over there,' he gestures towards a walled garden across the street in the broiling LA sunshine. A large black woman is sitting there, and when we get there, Alan starts talking to her.

'Hey lady, guess where he's from?' he points at me and continues without waiting for an answer, 'He's from England. He speaks English, but I can't understand a word he says.'

He turns to me,

'Say something, English.'

I am not a performing monkey, and so I pointedly ignore him, smoking my cigarette in the ridiculously hot Californian sun and watch passing traffic.

They soon get into a conversation about the foods their mothers used to cook for them, but I'm out of my depth on the names of these Deep South food stuffs. It's all a foreign language to me of grits and collard greens, Cajun dishes, and other childhood soul foods. I don't know what these things are, so I look at the bullion lorry with its police escort and smoke my tobacco, waiting for a heist to occur in front of me.

Eventually, it's just too hot for me, and I saunter off inside to cool down, leaving Alan with his new best friend. She was nice enough but lost points for admitting to being a creationist early on in the conversation. More than fifty per cent of this country believe in the seven day myth—scary, eh?

Well, I skulked around in the shadows (as you do), and eventually we exchanged our tickets for allocated seating from a lovely Amtrak employee called Kelsey.

I said to her with a weak smile,

'It's my first time on Amtrak.'

'Oh that's okay, sir,' she replied with a perfect smile and handed me my seating ticket. I looked at it incredulously.

'That says seat 13, carriage 13!'

'So it does.'

'Oh! Thanks a lot,' I replied in mock horror.

She laughed when she realised I was pulling her leg, but seriously, 'seat 13 in carriage 13?' This didn't bode well.

We continue to wait, tickets now in hand, for the gates to open and allow us to start the treasure hunt that promises a seat on the train. The hall is filled now with other train queues, milling cleaners, lost punters, and assorted oddballs. Then suddenly, through the general hub-bub: Ah yes. Make way people, make way; a double-sized golf buggy is forcing its way through the crowds and heading for us with Alan Flora sitting regally on the back waving to passers-by as he goes, doffing his hat to ladies that take his fancy. With a cheeky grin, he notices me staring in disbelief, and then he disappears into the crowd, gliding effortlessly towards the train.

I sat in my doomed seat on The Southwest Chief by the window, waiting to see what would happen. The long distance Amtrak trains all have names like this: The Texas Eagle, The Desert Wind, The Empire State Express, the St. Louis Mule, The Pacific Surfliner, and The Empire Builder. They even have one called The Wolverine that runs between Chicago and Pontiac. Its more to do with the routes than the actual trains having the names, but you can tell that somebody with passion was involved when they started naming things. Of course, it isn't a patch on our own atmospherically named West Coast Main Line, the splendour of our East Coast Main Line, and the adventurously named Cross Country Route. They don't call the United Kingdom 'the most romantic country just off the coast of Europe that's not called Ireland' for nothing, y'know.

[Oh lucky man in LA's Union Station]

There was nearly double the amount of leg room found on the Greyhound, with a fold-down table and foot rests like an aircraft (but notably far more room than I'd ever experienced on any aircraft). Far wider seats made for even more comfort. This was luxury already, and I was finally able to relax.

The first person who sat next to me was a mad old bat who had the wrong seat. I pointed this out to her, but she had to have that piece of information confirmed by an American accent before she'd actually believe it. Eventually, the mad old coot buggered off to her correct seat somewhere behind me. That was a close call. Whoever did take lucky seat number 14 in carriage 13 was going to spend a great deal of time in my company, and so we'd better get on. Unlike the Greyhound, these passengers were generally going all the way (so to speak), from the start to the end, without getting off along the way. It's more flight-like, I guess, but without the free drinks and hijackings.

While I was mulling this over, I was joined by a tall, grey haired gentleman with a moustache, which made me think of the 'Navy' for some reason. He looked a lot like Sam Elliott (the actor). His demeanour and his posture, though, suggested a retired military man. He completely ignored me and read a paperback with an intense interest that worried me a little. I didn't say anything to him, and as the train started moving, he suddenly put his book down and turned to face me with a warm smile. He introduced himself as Bill (Cousins, it later transpired), and we shook hands and started talking. Luckily, he turned out to be a great bloke to be sharing a seat with for forty-three hours between LA and Chicago, and I made a new friend.

Bill was about ten years older than me, but you'd never know it; he'd got a great sense of humour and a similar perspective on life (and the government, in particular). He had an easy warmth and an inquisitive mind, which was refreshing for me, after so long without a proper conversation.

Alan Flora was also on board carriage 13 (obviously), a few seats behind us, flirting with all the young women. I could hear his whispering charms even from where I sat.

. . . And the giggles that they elicited from their victims.

Throughout our journey, Alan, Bill, and I would meet up for a smoke on the side of the platform when the train pulled into a station, although Bill was a pipe smoker who was just starting out and didn't do cigarettes anymore, he'd still come out onto the concrete with us and chat amongst the smoke.

'Hey, English.'

'Hey Indy. How's it going, man?'

We'd holler at each other over the sound of the train, as Bill, (and others) looked on, surprised by our friendship (and possibly my accent). I guess we did look a strange gang; an old man in an off-white suit, like a faded Broadway star, a scruffy bearded punk, and Sam Elliott.

It was good to have some travelling companions, though, and Bill and I often shared a drink and some food. He kept trying to get me to eat, but I was on a reduced diet (through choice), and he couldn't get over how little sleep and food I needed. On the first night, he and I shared out his Jim Beam whiskey before dozing off. An old sailor, sat nearly opposite, offered to get his own bottle of rum and share it with us—it was quite a party atmosphere, with a Mexican biker from LA sitting behind us telling all and sundry about his Vietnam experience.

'If I go through airport security butt naked, I'd still set off the alarms with the amount of shrapnel I've got in me. Hahaha.'

He basically told us his whole life story over two days, and it wasn't too boring; he worked with computers (I know, I know) but was a field agent and went to his jobs on his Harley, all leathered up and wearing a Nazi WW2 helmet. Scared the shit out of every customer, but was so good at his job, his boss didn't mind.

The sailor was an old fella, forty years a captain for other people's yachts and master of his own. He was full of himself, but when he overheard me and Bill, offered the rum and later, when he heard I was a writer, came over to show me on his cell phone his wife's quilting artwork (for some unexplained reason). I 'ooed' and 'ahhhed' at all the right places, and he seemed satisfied when he returned to his seat. We never saw the bottle of rum, but undoubtedly, he would've let us have some if we'd have pushed him. Later on though, I saw a darker, crueller side to him when we were all trying to get to sleep. The Mexican computer biker was still talking about Vietnam, and the sailor went over to him and hissed with real venom in his tone,

'Every time I try to go to sleep, I hear you talking about Vietnam. Then I start dreaming about it. So can you just shut up about it now, so we can get some sleep?'

I don't know if the sailor had been in it too (he could have been, judging from his age), but the Mexican then sloped off to the bar for a few hours and didn't come back until everyone else was asleep. He must've talked himself out by 11.30PM.

His stories hadn't bothered me, but I think the prejudices I witnessed towards Mexicans on my journeys made me wonder about Americans. Outside of the USA, we all seem to have the impression that white Americans treat black Americans badly, when it actually appears to be that Mexicans are the lowest of the low in status now. It doesn't matter where you go from lowlife to high; the Mexican is the fall guy in America. It's disturbing. I tried to fight my middle class guilt and not over compensate.

[My first sighting of the Mississippi was on the train.]

Tuesday 5th June 2012

ALBUQUERQUE (NM)
{NOT MUNCHING}

KANSAS CITY (MO)
{MEN ONLY}

My initial impressions on Amtrak comfort, much like my arse, has taken a battering:

> *Sleep was almost impossible what with the seats being like rocks, the vibration from the train, the constant hoot of the horn, the doors opening between carriages as people walked through, the farts of old men, and the snoring of those already oblivious to the sound of Amtrak.*

Bill asked me in the morning,
'I'm going to wash my hair. Would you like some of my shampoo?'
'Nah, I'm okay,' I replied.
'Well, I don't mind feeling bad inside, as long as I look good outside.'
'What are you saying?' I say, raising an eyebrow in mock insult.
'Nothing,' he sniggers.
'Git!'
There were lots of good natured comments and conversations like that throughout the journey. If I saw him in a queue of people or not paying for something quickly enough, I'd call out,
'Oi Bill, come on, ya tight wad!'

Okay, so it wasn't exactly Oscar Wilde, perhaps you had to be there.

But Bill was cool. He would've made a great friend, I think. The only down side I could see with Bill was that he quite liked exercise (hiking) and believed in that creationist crap. Other than that, I reckon we could get along. His eyes lit up when I told him about our bohemian pub group of writers and musicians back home, and he spoke about how he'd love to live in a pub culture like ours, but America just didn't do that sort of thing. I suggested he start one of his own, but he didn't sound convinced.

People started to leave the train from our original group, and as new ones took their place, they became part of our gang.

Throughout our journey, the pretty Amtrak employee, Kelsey, had been our carriage girl, staying with us, laughing and chatting, making sure everyone was happy. It was a nice touch that made all the difference to the time we spent on the train. Every so often, she'd come through the length of the train calling out for a missing passenger by the name of Johnny McDonald. The first time she got to our carriage and asked about the whereabouts of the mystery passenger, the sailor answered,

'I can be Johnny McDonald for you, if you'd like?'

This caused the carriage and Kelsey to laugh out loud. After a few more calls for Johnny, he started to become our response to any announcement.

'We will be ten minutes late into Flagstaff.'

'That'll be that bloody Johnny McDonald driving then!'

'The dining car will be open in half an hour.'

'I bet that Johnny McDonald'll be at the front of the queue!'

When a male guard came through and asked the question, he was startled when the whole carriage burst out laughing at him. Confused and muttering to himself, he turned on his heel and headed back the way he'd come, to the sound of our cheers. Kelsey appeared later and scolded us with a smirk, having had to apologise on our behalf.

Downstairs (for this was a double decker train) was Chip, who ran the snack bar, playing rockabilly music on the stereo as he served beer and other bits and bobs. He was funny after he got to know us and our habits and was happy to give us free refills for our coffee (which wasn't standard on the train). I always tipped but noticed that others didn't, not even the coins in their change, the tight bastards. I think he appreciated our company, as we didn't just buy and bugger off; we stayed to chat and have a laugh.

The main steward who ran the dining car was amazing. The first time we heard his voice over the intercom he said,

'Hi there! I'm the famous Sam, and I run the dining car.'

He sounded like Waylon Smithers from the Simpsons.

'Hi there again! It's me, Sam; the person that Kelsey hates most on this train . . . '

And,

'Hi there folks! It's the world famous Sam here—how are you all doing?'

I never ate in the diner, it was too expensive for me, but I enjoyed the announcements immensely. It was all so theatrical. It felt like a chorus line would appear at any minute or a conga line would spontaneously form. The forty-three hours on that train zipped by.

Day one had taken us from Los Angeles to a place called Needles (straddling the California/Arizona boarder), through the Mojave Desert (home of Death Valley), and further into Arizona to Flagstaff (home of the Lowell Observatory). Unlike the Greyhound before, air conditioned carriages saved us from the ridiculous heat outside. In the past, pointless fact fans, Needles has recorded the highest temperatures in the whole world. So now you know, try dropping that into conversations.

By day two we had passed the Grand Canyon (not close enough to see anything on this line, but there is a bus link to the Grand Canyon Railway from Williams Junction) and across the San Francisco Peaks, Canyons (Padre & Diabalo), across the Little Colorado River, into New Mexico, and onto the Red Rock State Park (not the location of that U2 album—that's in Colorado).

I pointed out some tumbleweed to Bill; it was the first I'd ever seen in the flesh, so to speak.

'That's nothing. I saw a tumbleweed the size of a VW back in LA when I was a kid. We called them 'LA snowballs.' You don't wanna get hit by one!'

Albuquerque got short measure from our Mexican biker;

'It's a shit hole! There's nothing there. It's shit!'

A little voice piped up in reply from somewhere behind us at the back of the carriage,

'Hey mister, there's kids here too!'

'It's still a shit hole.'

I forgot to mention the God squad behind us all; a little girl aged around the eleven/twelve mark and her grandfather (who had brought her up, apparently, judging by the overheard conversations that I tried to ignore) were all over themselves with godly references (and by that, I don't mean they kept mentioning ex-members of the pop group 10cc).

'I'm starting to read my Bible now,' said the little girl in a sparkly T-shirt with a CND symbol on it.

'Oh, and where are you up to?' asks a female voice, obviously sat nearby.

'John.'

'Oh that's a good one.'

'Yeah. I'm really getting it. I like John.'

I've got to say, she was extremely well behaved and mature, but I was worried about the brainwashing that was going on.

'What's damnation?' she asked at one point.

'Oh, you're talking about the final day, when we get judged,' replied her grandfather, after a pause.

'She'll be fine; she's a pure soul. She's been brought up good,' said a new male voice.

'Thank you, sir.'

You could hear the smile in the grandfather's voice.

'But what happens?' asked the child again.

'Oh, you don't have to worry 'bout that, dear. Loads have predicted it, but they've all been wrong, honey.'

And with that, the conversation went quiet, and I think I drifted off, but that might've been boredom and not tiredness.

The little girl's grandfather sported the standard white moustache of a believer, blank T-shirt, blue jeans, and baseball cap. 'Good solid folk,' as they're often referred to in the press (or 'simple folk,' if you prefer).

So, New Mexico, across the Continental Divide, where more mountains and canyons appear and pass as our journey continues through Lamy (home of 137 people, thirty-seven sheepies, and three little piggies), followed by a completely different and unrelated Las Vegas, Raton, and Trinidad (hang on, where the hell are we going? Oh, Trinidad in Colorado—phew). Fleetingly, we pass through Dodge City in Kansas, the home of the OK Corral of Wyatt Earp and Doc Holiday fame. I admit, I got a little frisson of excitement as we did that, due to my upbringing on all things 'cowboy.' America does this to you all the time. We've spent our entire lives being fed their culture through all forms of media, and so it feels weird when you actually see it in the flesh.

The locations change, but the faces on the train remain the same. Something had changed, though, and the sky was suddenly filled with clouds; we even had a raindrop hit us for a second. The landscape was frighteningly flat, featureless, and deadly. No obvious shelter from the sun burning your brains, no water supplies, and not an animal to be seen. Empty fields, the odd deer here and there, but where were all the cattle? I think I counted six horses between LA and Chicago, and one of those was tethered to a car wing mirror outside a shack.

[The Tripods are coming]

There were decrepit shacks aplenty. When I asked him, Bill reckoned they were probably Indian reservation homes, but I wasn't so sure. There were too many of them scattered over all different terrain and distances. I reckoned it was poor white trash. Well that's the only humans I saw outside, if anybody at all. I never saw a Native-American anywhere near these corrugated shit holes. I wonder if Albuquerque is full of these hovels?

Kansas City (KS)
{KINKY SEX}

Chicago (IL)
{INSIDE LAMAS}

Kansas City (KS)—you're a great song and a great place to get off a train and have a cigarette. I love you, Kansas City; everything you could ever want from an ashtray—sunshine and warm air.

Chicago (IL) was in our sights now, and everyone was beginning to get excited again and anxious not to miss their connections. An Italian man sat next to us across the aisle, in a blue baseball cap, specs, blue shirt, and blue shorts (ensemble by blind man at C&A). He was constantly talking loudly on his mobile phone quite rudely and without consideration for the rest of us. He couldn't understand Kelsey's explanations about time delays, how the company allows extra time over long distances, and that we'd be in on time.

And then a big, fat Texan got on with his wife;

'Celebratin' our fiftieth wedding anniversary,' he informed nobody in particular.

If he'd had two six-shooters, he'd probably have peppered the ceiling with a loud 'Yee Ha!'

They seemed jolly enough, until God turned up in conversation (he's bloody omnipresent, isn't he?). A black bloke and a young Latino boxer had joined them in the seats ahead, and they quickly got into conversation as if they already knew each other. The black bloke spoke very smooth and slowly like a Mormon—well trained/ practiced and more than slightly creepy. His philosophy was all home spun shit, which went down well with the old Texans—all 'momma's shortbread' shit and lessons learnt from sitting on their grandma's knees. He seemed about my age, and I didn't respect him at all, until later, I found out he was the father of a forty-three-year-old and a seven year old son(clearly NOT my age, then). His eldest son does respect him by not smoking in front of him, but he told him that he'd rather see him dead in a car crash than to know he's smoking, or 'doin' that stuff to himself,' but when he started on, I thought his son was some sort of deadbeat junkie. He and the Texan had been boxers, so that's why they were hanging out with the young Latino.

> *After Missouri (MO), we quickly travelled through Iowa (IA), and near the border with Illinois, finally came to the great Mississippi River—that wide expanse of brown water and sludge. It was impressive, though. It's the bloody spelling joke/actual flippin' river—you've got to love it, if you love American literature. Mark Twain—you are a god.*

Illinois (IL) brings us Galesburg, Princeton, Mendota, and Naperville, before we finally break up the old gang at Chicago. I wanted to shout 'Johnny McDonald!' one more time, so I left it until we all hit the platforms then gave it a go. Most people looked to see what all the fuss was about, except the members of carriage thirteen. High fives struck the air, and like Spartacus before him— Johnny McDonald's name shall live forever, as it echoed through the railway station at Chicago. Or perhaps not.

It was strange to be ending part of our journey here. Who would continue with me to New York City? Well, I knew that God's family were on the way, because she'd said quite loudly on the train. It turned out the Latino boxer was also set for the city, but I didn't know that until later. At this point, Bill and I went off to find his favourite tobacconist in Chicago. He didn't say too much about it as we trooped through the glorious sunshine and against the flow of homeward bound workers flooding across the streets. A few left turns, a right, and then here we are at 195 Wabash Ave.—the home of Iwan Ries & Co. of Chicago, America's oldest family owned tobacco shop:

> Started in 1857, just twenty years after the incorporation of Chicago, and four years before the Civil War, German immigrant Edward Hoffman established a small tobacco shop, E. Hoffman & Co., in Chicago's famous Sherman House hotel.
>
> As business grew Edward realized that he could not run it alone. In 1891, he recruited his nephew, Iwan Ries, from Germany and the second generation had begun.
>
> Now on its fifth generation, Iwan Ries & Co. is also the home of The Iwan Ries Lounge, downtown Chicago's only smoking lounge. After the smoking ban they converted some old warehouse space into 'the most comfortable space for smokers' in Chicago.

Says some online spiel from the company website (iwanries. com), however, from the street, there was hardly a sign of what I was about to experience. The entrance was a nondescript door in a granite façade, which led to some stairs. Bill led the way, up a flight of stairs, past an open door showing empty leather bound chairs in a large wood panelled room, to the single door of the shop. Inside was a central island that the five or six staff stood behind, and circling them upon every inch of the wall space were millions of pipes, cigars, lighters, hookahs, and every other smoking related item you could imagine. They didn't sell any cigars from Cuba obviously, but everything else, including a few green ones (which I hadn't seen since the Bahamas). I needed some rolling tobacco, and the bloke, who served me the nearest I could find to my normal brand, then surprised me by saying,

'You gonna try it then? You can use any ashtray.'

He gestured towards the many lying around on the work surfaces, which had so far escaped my eyes. Was this bloke actually suggesting that I light up now, inside his shop? Well, yes he was. It was the weirdest feeling—walking around, smoking a cigarette, whilst looking at other smoking stuff. Not having to be concerned that people might be breathing in your smoke accidently. I kept expecting the cops to rush in and bust us, like in the speakeasy days. I took a rare photo of myself in the shop—they'd never believe this back at home.

[Smoking inside a tobacco shop!]

After Bill had got the stuff he wanted, we headed back to the Union Station, where his connection was going to be in about an hour's time. Mine wasn't until 9.30PM, so we parted, wished each other well, and split. To keep myself alive I took in a beer at the station bar, some gumbo fish stuff from an angry Chinese food stall, and a few more cigarettes up top. Eventually, I returned to find a massive queue. Quickly, I fell into line, and by 9.30PM, we were on our twenty-hour journey to New York City on the Lake Shore Limited train numbered 48.

This time I had a double chair to myself; it wasn't allocated seating, so perhaps I was getting scruffy enough and smell too bad for some folk. I do hope so. I haven't brushed my teeth in three days, and my bum is not my best feature either! I'm looking forward to having a shave and getting cleaned up in NYC.

Fell into a fitful sleep after taking a painkiller pill than numbed my numb bum, number.

[Views from a moving train]

Thursday 7th June 2012

CHICAGO (IL)
[IT LEAKS]

NEW YORK CITY (NY)
[NOB YETI]

Not exactly great views on this leg of the journey; apart from the lack of 'actual' views, due to me being on the wrong side of the train (it's all lumberyards and cliff sides), my seat was also between windows, so I got half a view at all times. The carriage was too full for me to change to another seat, so I had to put up with it. No matter; New York tonight.

No Bill or Alan, in fact, the whole journey from Chicago was uneventful, quiet, and considerably less entertaining. The friendliness of the previous journey was replaced by silences and headphones.

Pulling out of Chicago, we crossed the border into Indiana and passed through Gary (IN). I never thought I'd pass through Gary (and in a train!), but there you have it; that's what we did.

No-one sat next to me the whole time—I reckon my body odour put them off. I had a full white beard, without brushing my teeth for three days or clothes. I can only imagine how dirty I smelt. Tough shit folks, that's life on the road. It's not that big a deal, I'm not trying to make any friends here.

In front of me were a couple of young girls, one with blonde hair tied in a ponytail, the other had dark hair. I assumed (correctly as it turned out), to be oriental, and she slept for most of the journey.

I could only see her hair poking through between our seats and by the window most of the way.

> *Flirting is like good manners—it's worth practicing, just take it for what it is; it's not a chat up. If you are settled, it's still good exercise. Love is good, but love of your life is fabulous. I am a lucky man. I'll never forget that.*

So, although my body found another body attractive, I did nothing, except got her case down for her (it was large) (steady!), and then hit New York again.

I love New York. If I could stay here forever, I'd be the happiest man in the country. This is a fabulous city, full of the great and the good. Everything breathes in NYC. It's the lungs of the USA. Total control. I can see why Strummer loved it here. And Lennon, come to think of it. This vibrant place beats, it really does, like a heart. Nothing stops, nothing is impossible, and nothing means anything here. Your future is happening in the present—create your reality. Nobody is a nobody here. I love NYC!

I was looking forward to seeing Kara again and showing her the review of my book in *Ugly Things Magazine*.

[back on the train]

Come breakfast time, a call went out and I decided to end my train journey with a meal on the train, so I walked back to the carriage behind us, and when they had established that I was alone, I was directed to a table for four where a single man sat. He was older than me, perhaps in his late fifties, with glasses and a lived in face. I sat diagonally and said hello. His name was Joe, and his profession was stunt co-ordinator for the Hollywood film industry. We started out talking about my love of the Ford Mustang, and he told me of just one of a lifetime's stunts he'd been involved in.

'We had to drive a train into a Ford Mustang with Lou Diamond Phillips in it. So we put some train wheels on the car and then tied a cable under the car and ran it under the train. Then, instead of the train hitting the car, we pulled the car into the train. By then, of course, we had a dummy in the car, instead of Lou Diamond Phillips.'

He told me of his life and how he seemed to always be in

demand, how he worked seventy-two hour weeks, week in, week out, relentlessly at the beck and call of the studios. Pushing himself to the physical limit, trying to fulfil their demands. Sleep deprivation and physical activity don't lend themselves to safety much, but he was lucky enough, or just damn good at his job, that he never got killed.

I liked Joe. Retired now, he had a relaxed attitude about him that radiated satisfaction. He saved up $80K and retired and then had the pleasure of being able to turn down requests for him to return. It sounded like he was a big wheel, but you never can tell with passing ships. Still, we laughed together as we were joined by other single men at our table, and I couldn't think of a better way to start the day. The food was excellent (five-star restaurant quality, not the crap you get on British trains), and the atmosphere was warm. I had my first ever blini (a Russian pancake), and they were fabulous, although probably more calories than I'd had in the last three days combined, and then we returned to our seats for the leg into New York, and Boston for Joe. The train separated, and half of it went onto Boston, while we turned left and down towards Manhattan and our final destination of Penn Station.

I was on the wrong side of the train to see the river as we slid through the countryside, but one expanse of water is much like another, I suppose. A few bridges and we started to get into an urban landscape again. I started to feel excited about the fact, and suddenly I didn't want to be on that train any longer. I wanted to be walking the streets of New York again, feeling the heat, smelling the food wafting around me, and above all, hearing the sounds of millions of people vibrating with life as they passed. The train became quite stale and alien after three days, and the people became quiet within as the atmosphere rose amongst us. Conversations stopped, as we could all see familiar views and noted sights. The odd comment spoke for all our thoughts and hung in the air like community clouds raining down in the carriage.

Tanoys (apparently like 'Hoovers,' turns out to be a manufacturer's name and not the object, so no-one in America knows what they are) crackled with messages about our final destination. The humorous comments all exchanged for vital information involving timings and connections. For some of us, there was no more track, and when the train stopped, so did we.

For others, of course, this was just another inconvenience, as they hunted down their next train to take them forward on their own personal journeys. Mine was nearly over. Anticipation now mixed with sadness at the impending finale. I contemplated my place within my surroundings and tried to place myself in New York City.

Finally, our train crawled to a halt, and I slipped off onto the platform, dodging slow moving passengers and headed towards every sign that read 'exit.' Up some stairs, away from the artificial light of the station and out into the city.

Noise hits me first and then the air, as I stepped up onto Penn Street. People milled around me, and I searched for a taxi. Nothing happening man. So I did what I hadn't done in three days; I walked. It was only about seven or eight blocks from the Hotel Carter, anyway, and I needed to fit in again, so I was fine with my choice. The humidity quickly took effect, and I was sweating by the fourth block. Perhaps I was walking too fast, but I didn't mind; I was heading for my hotel, a shower, and a large bed to lie on. Heaven was within my grasp.

Eventually, I started to get close and recognised some of the shops. 40, 41, 42, and then there she was: 43rd and my awaiting bed.

I strolled up the block and into the foyer, part of me expecting a round of applause, but instead, I had to wait for a slow thinking couple to check in, before I was allowed to do the same.

'Hello again,' I said to the gentleman behind the desk.

'Hello.'

'I was in 707 about a week or two ago. Don't suppose I could have the same room, could I?'

He checks. I wait.

'Ahh, sorry, that's taken,' but seeing my disappointment, he gives me 753, which he assures me is a lovely room. (It isn't. It's right next to the lifts, and I can hear them go 'ping' every time someone gets in or out on the seventh floor.)

I go up and change, sort of. I have the same jeans I've had on for three weeks, the same socks I've had on for four days. (I'm scared to take them off, in case I can't face putting them back on again.) So I change my shirt, wash my hair, grab my biker's jacket, and head out for some food. It's around 5.30PM now, and Smiths Bar is full of eating folk, so I head for the New York Brewing Co. and find Kara isn't working today (no matter). I plonk myself at the bar next to

a smartly suited gent and start drinking the beers. He's excited by
the basketball game on the TV. It's the Celtic somebodies playing
the Miami somebody elses. It looks good, and he's rooting for the
Celtics, so I do too. They lose.

Somehow we end up in conversation (businessman and leather
jacketed, long hair, in a meeting of minds). Quickly, he tells me he's
divorced, now three years, and wants to know where all the girls
are. I jokingly say that it must be me that's putting them off and
stand to let the mythical hordes arrive. Slowly he starts to direct his
conversation away from me, and I decide to move on.

It's closer to nine thirty now, and I'm exhausted, but I have
to walk past Birdland to get home, and as is my want in these
situations, I decide to go in and see some live jazz (8.30—11pm).
Its thirty dollars to get in, but that includes a drink at the bar. I
choose Charlie Parker's favourite cocktail. I can't remember what it
was called, but it tasted like a margarita with key lime pie in it and
tasted lovely. My biker's jacket and long hair stuck out, so I hung at
the bar and chatted to my 'server,' Chris. He's cool enough to let me
have a load of Birdland matches to take home as souvenirs, while he
pours me a fabulous margarita and gets me a plate of skewers. The
skewers involved meat, as far as I can recall, but apart from them
tasting delicious, I can't give you any more information. Next up
was a martini, and boy that boy can make a martini. It was fantastic.
The best I've ever had. (Coincidently, the only one I've ever had
made for me.)

The music had started by now and Karrin Allyson, apparently,
"this era's premier hot/cool jazz kitten/composer,"(!) was singing
mellow tunes with her band. She was attempting to create a sublime
atmosphere in the historic club, but I knew I was going to have to
head home though, and because it was ten thirty, I was on my last
legs. I mooched over to the merchandise stall and tried to purchase
some trinkets. I was whispering, but even that got me told off. I
finally got a badge, and I think at that point I was asked to leave. I
recall it being a mutual decision by all the other patrons, and I've
got to say, they were probably right. And in point of fact, they were
way too precious about what was actually nothing amazing. It was
very middle of the road, background jazz that wouldn't have been
out of place (ironically) on a Manhattan Transfer album. I probably
shouldn't have gone in there drunk and proceed to get drunker, but

I was on a limited time budget and had a whole stack of things to get through.

The next thing I had to get through, in particular, was back in the Hotel Carter and involved my feet. Oh lovely; how they stunk. I washed them in the sink and then fell asleep in the lovely, extremely large bed in Room 753. 'I love this place,' I thought, as I shut my eyes.

Friday 8th June 2012

New York City . . .

My last full day in the city. Tomorrow I would be flying home, and today was all mine.

New York—home of the baseball cap wearing individual. I got up and headed for the lift. It was full when it stopped at my floor, but after watching a second lift finally appear full and continue its way downwards without me, I climbed into the third one that opened its doors to me. This was packed too, but there was enough room for me to squeeze in. The stairs had alluded me as I waited between lifts, so it was a lift or nothing. The doors shut behind me. Nothing happened for a while. The numbers on the wall didn't move, and then finally, we edged down. We stopped again. The doors opened halfway between floors and shut again. Nothing happened. Some people started to get nervous and hit the alarm button. A distorted voice spoke through the tiny speaker, but no-one replied in the lift as the doors opened again and a couple of nervous women took their chances and leapt up onto the floor that was probably six or five. The doors shut once more, and we all started moving down again. At the lobby, we all got out as if nothing had happened. When I returned later, there were paper signs stuck on all the lift doors in the lobby, reminding us that only eight people maximum should be in the lifts at any one time. I think we had about twelve in ours that morning (plus luggage). I didn't feel an ounce of fear. I think my journey had given me a mental suit of armour against all danger. I had completed this amazing journey, how could a mere lift stop me now?

My feet took me directly to Smiths Bar and a table in the restaurant, where my morning 'full Irish' and black coffee was dispensed by a lovely black lady with a smile and an expansive cleavage. She opened up the wall of windows onto 8th Avenue as I ate my favourite breakfast in my favourite first stop bar in the city. The sun was starting to shine down the streets, and all was fresh. Fouteen dollars, including toast and water (if requested) was a bargain in my books. Smiles, warmth, and a sense of belonging received, I went out for a cigarette or two before returning to the bar to have a few Bud Lites from Mike, the barman with more than a touch of the Ted Danson about him. He is such a good bloke. I'd chatted with him before I left for LA, and I wasn't sure if he'd remembered me, so I stayed for a few bottles, between cigarettes outside, safe in the knowledge that my precious beaten up leather jacket would still be at the bar with my wallet inside it.

While outside on the corner of 44th West and 8th, I got asked for directions a couple of times as I had a smoke. I always take that as a sign that you fit in; when people think you look like a local. Eventually, I needed a shave and so headed back to the room to clean my face of nearly three weeks' growth. It took six Bic razors and no hot water. After a little while, I was ready to return to the NYBC on 44th West, where Kara would be behind the bar again. Sure enough, as I walked through the door, I heard her voice call out, 'Hey! Look who's back!' and suddenly I felt at home. As my eyes became accustomed to the gloom, I saw her grinning at me from behind the bar and a sheepish smile played across my face.

'Hey Kara!'

I brought out the review copy of *Ugly Things Magazine* and gave it to her across the wood as she served me my first pint. I think part of it was me showing off, part of it was wanting her to know that I was a real writer and part of it was a genuine pride in what I'd done. The review wasn't 100% praise, which I take to be a better informed opinion than one which merely sees one side of the coin.

We chatted for ages, she served others, but always came straight back to me for some more tales of travel. I think if I lived in NYC, we'd probably be friends. Maybe not. Anyway, after a few hours, I had to go and see Johnny at the Russian, and although I didn't want to leave her company, we said goodbye, and she came out from behind the bar and gave me a big hug. It didn't feel right to kiss her, so I just held her for a few seconds and then we parted. I'll miss her.

I headed out to the Firebird restaurant. As I turned the corner of the block, Johnny saw me and called out, 'Hey, Alex!' We hugged as we met, and he added, 'I didn't think I'd see you again, man.'

I told him I needed to pop in to the House of the Brews, but I'd be back in a minute. As I walked down the steps next door, Johnny introduced me to the female owner, as a good friend of his, to which she instantly bought me a drink. I paid for a second and put a fifty dollars next to it and told the bar staff I owed it to Alison. I'm sure I was out of order last time. They questioned me, and I assured them with a quick description of her. Eventually, she came forward, bewildered by this money. She claimed I was okay last time I visited, but I insisted she had the money as a tip.

Later, I spoke to her without an audience of her colleagues, and she assured me I was fine. I still feel bad, but if nothing else, it proves chucking money at things rarely makes them better. I left feeling I'd done the right thing, however, and met up with Johnny on the street above.

We chatted for ages, and then I told him I was going in to his restaurant (it wasn't his—he just worked the door there). He took me down the stairs and, again, gave me a massive introduction to the receptionist, who was waiting to seat the customers. I felt like royalty in this poshest of posh restaurants (although I looked like an old Ramone). This was a five-star establishment, where only the top people ate. I took a table near to the kitchen in the nearly empty room. I didn't mind; it was only me eating, and I did look a bit scruffy. I'm surprised they didn't demand to see the colour of my money before I sat down. A few groups started to take their tables around me, and you could smell the money. You could see it in their clothes and their demeanour. They didn't look down at me; in fact, they hardly appeared to notice me at all. But my money was as good as theirs, and I ordered the most expensive vodka on the menu ($24 a shot!). The starter was cocked up, because I ordered something that was meant for two, so I had to re-order some gravlax instead, (very good), and then I asked the waiter to ask the chef to choose my main course, which he did. Although I have no idea what it was now (it involved meat of some sort), it was lovely and surprisingly filling. I paid up (best part of $100) and hit the street. Probably took no more than three-quarters of an hour in all, and most of that was waiting to be served, but it was good food and another experience I could tick off the list. If ever I came into serious money, I would certainly eat there again, but otherwise, it was just too pricey for my usual wage packet.

I stood with Johnny, and we chatted as I smoked. Later, I left him, still working the pavement, a new friend that one day I would meet again.

The day was coming to an end for me, although not for everyone else. It was only early evening, but I wanted to get back to the hotel room, do some writing, and get a good night's sleep. Tomorrow would be a lot of travelling, and I really wanted to ring home to hear everyone's voices.

Alone in the room, I tried to suck it all in; the journey, the atmosphere, the feeling of belonging in this place that had been with me the minute I'd spoken to the American customs man a few weeks ago. It still felt like I was in a movie somehow, but now the credits were starting to roll. Turning out the light, I listened to the city seven stories below as it continued to vibrate. My last night in New York.

Saturday 9th June 2012

New York City (NY)
{NEARLY YOUNG}

Deathrow (UK) . . .
{UNDER KWIK-I-MART}

Check out by noon left me with a quandary—what the hell was I gonna do until my flight at 9PM tonight? I didn't want to follow myself by going to a bar somewhere and getting drunk again, as I did when killing time at the start of this journey. I certainly wasn't going to schlep around the city sightseeing, so I decided to head for the airport after midday and spend the last few hours in JFK. Maybe at a bar.

So I got sorted in the room, packed all I could fit in the bag, and went out for a final breakfast at Smiths bar. I sat at a table and had my usual order (Irish full traditional breakfast). Mike was serving and saw me as he walked past my table.

'Hey! How's it going? You been served?'

He shook my hand and paused beside me.

'Yeah, no worries,' I replied, although I felt glum knowing what I did.

'Good to see you.'

And as he passed on, he put one hand upon my right shoulder in a friendly gesture.

He had no idea what I was going through internally about leaving. It was really beginning to cut me up, and that small, insignificant gesture nearly pushed me over the edge. I almost broke down completely. Luckily, being English trained, I was able to maintain a sense of self and bit hard onto my lip instead.

Breakfast was as excellent as ever, fourteen dollars, and so I left twenty to cover a tip. Then outside for a smoke or two and back into the bar for a Bud Lite. I took the corner seat again, and Mike was quick to serve. There were other customers watching a game on the telly. Manly men making noise. I kept myself to myself, mourning my fate, nursing a bottle. Occasionally, I'd pop out for a smoke and as always, leaving my jacket/wallet on the back of my seat. It felt safe in Smiths Bar. It felt safe in Manhattan. In fact, I never felt scared or even mildly worried anywhere in the States—it just isn't like that if you have an open mind and an ounce of common sense. Not everyone does.

The bottles of Bud Lite were four dollars this morning, so with the standard dollar tip, we're talking five bucks a pop (about £3), which is amazing for a major city. In London you'd expect to pay over £5 for a bottle in any pub. Anyway, without so much fuss I had a couple of bottles, left the money on the bar (as is traditional), and a twenty dollar tip. I wanted to stay, but I needed to do some gift shopping for the kids and needed to beat that noon deadline.

A couple of blocks down (41st?) was a shop selling NYPD and NYFD T-shirts that I'd seen earlier on the way to the bus station, and sure enough, it was full of tourist tat, the like of which I wouldn't normally touch. But this was for the kids, I told myself, as I bought toy yellow cabs and school buses (ten dollars each) for Jess and some T-shirts, metal number plates, mini Statues of Liberty, and a million dollar pencil case for Julie and Sam.

I'd like to have bought some more, but my bag was pretty full already, and I'd travelled so light I hadn't any room for anything else. As it was, I had to leave one of my T-shirts behind in the hotel room once everything was packed. (It was an old one, but even so.)

Back to the hotel room, I had a while to kill and so watched the French Open women's final on the telly, laughing at the grunts the two women made every time they hit the ball. The winner shouted, 'Ugh!' every time she connected, while the loser of the match, a French girl half the winner's size and seriously outplayed (ranked 15 against the winner ranked 2), shouted something that sounded exactly like 'LOSER!' It was hilarious. I'm sure it was either just a sound effect or perhaps a French word I didn't know (there are so many!), but it sounded so like 'LOSER!' that I couldn't stop watching. I expected someone to step onto the court and tell her to stop it, but nobody did, and the insults continued to the bitter and predictable end. At that point, the men's final was due to start, and I was due to leave the room. I left my loose change for the cleaner, as I always do, and quite a lot of bathroom things, like shampoo, toothpaste, razors, and even a bottle of painkillers that I'd got for the bus journey.

I had to queue to checkout (I hate that—why can't we fast track our way out? We're only dropping our pass-cards) and hit the streets. I was going nowhere. Leaning up against the hotel, I had a couple of cigarettes and then sauntered over to the crowd of yellow cab drivers that always filled the sidewalk.

'Okay . . . ' I got their attention 'who wants to go to JFK?' (It's a fixed rate, fifty-dollar ride.) The lucky driver ushered me into the back of his cab, and away we went, weaving through the midday traffic.

It's a set fee journey from Manhattan ($45 plus tip) and usually takes about thirty to forty minutes, depending on traffic and your starting point. I watched the city retreat behind me and marvelled at the cars and trucks around us. As we left Manhattan, I noticed the more ugly, but also more real suburbs of (Jersey?) as they lined the freeway. There was a lot less money here, and you could tell easily that this was not a tourist destination on anyone's list.

The young black driver got us to JFK quickly and pulled up at the entrance. The trunk opened so I could get my luggage out before I'd even got out the cab.

'Hey, I don't have any luggage man,' I said as I handed over the fee.

'Oh yeah, sorry,' he replied with a sheepish smile. My lack of luggage had thrown a few people along the way, but this was the first time with a cabbie. I got out in front of a Stalin-esque concrete building with no discernible features, bar a couple of automatic doors, a couple of bell hops, and a security guard. I asked the guard where I could smoke, and he indicated across the road, about as far away from him as I could be and yet still be in JFK. I sat on the wall and smoked a couple and then trooped inside. It was a grey day, but still not raining, the planes were noisily taking off and landing everywhere, and all I could think about was what all those normal Americans would be doing on a Saturday afternoon like this. Probably a ball game of some sort, shopping, all the usual stuff. I started to miss home. I was committed to this part of the journey now. America was behind me. I wasn't happy.

Inside the cavernous building, a woman showed me how to print my ticket out using my passport, and I headed for passport control. It took a long time to get through the metal detector section, but I didn't mind, as I had nothing but time at this point. The woman in front of me had a lot of luggage and placed one bag on the conveyor belt and then started to open it.

'Oh good,' I thought, 'This will slow us down.'

But then she stuck her hands inside and pulled out a large ginger cat. The bags all went through, and the cat and its owner walked on through the metal detector. She rehoused him on the other side when the magic metal detector wand had been waved around them both, and on it went.

A collection of Asian pre-teen girls, a father, and a son caused chaos with their inability to understand what was required of them at this point, and the queue started to build up. No priority boarding here, sunbeam.

Eventually, I was through and re-shoed, re-belted, and when fully dressed, was allowed on my not-so-merry way.

The terminal had been changed ('re-vamped' I imagine they call it), and none of the things we'd used (shops and the like) were where they had been last time we came to NYC (about a year previously). I found another gift shop and bought Sam another T-shirt (twenty-four dollars) (which, when I got home, turned out to not fit her) and tried to find a book on Bukowski. I tried a few shops, in fact, I tried all of them in the terminal, and not one copy of any of his books. I ended up with a Steve Earle novel called something like *I'll never get out of this world alive*. It was hard work, a little Burroughs mixed with Salinger, but not bad. Unfortunately, I was in a Hemmingway frame of mind with this journey.

I went looking for the section where I would board my flight in about eight hours. It was the furthest away, which suited me fine.

I sat in the moulded seat at the edge of the area and pulled the book out. The airport was quiet at this time (early afternoon), but passengers still wandered around looking lost and trying to sort themselves out. I dozed after a while and was woken by a large black guy sitting next to me and plugging in his laptop. He apologised for waking me when he saw me stirring and then plugged himself in and proceeded to listen to overtly loud dance music that I couldn't fail to hear. It was like a large scale Walkman situation. I went off for a drink. The only bar in town was a sports side bar. Crap style, crap service, and crap atmosphere. I left after one drink and left no tip, due to the shit service. It was a fucking disgrace in a country that prides itself on its service industry. The bar woman completely ignored me for about half an hour before finally serving me, and so I felt she deserved nothing. There was nothing worth eating here either, so I returned to my seat. The area was beginning to fill up around me at this point. Eventually, I thought this might be my flight leaving early and checked with the crew, but it was just another flight due out an hour before mine. Slowly the passengers filed out onto the plane until it was only me and the black guy left.

'You off to London?' he asked in a British accent. The only one I'd heard, so far, all the other passengers had been American or European (French, Italian etc.).

'Yeah, but not on this flight.'

'Well, good luck to you, man,' he smiled.

'And you,' I returned his smile.

He got up and ambled over to the check in, clearly not concerned with the fact that last call had been called half an hour ago and that the place was deserted.

That taught me a lesson: The plane won't be leaving faster if you queue up like a lemming, and the queue always takes ages to board anyway, so why stand when you can sit? Your seat will still be empty when you get on board.

The crew saw me watching.

'You enjoying this chaos?' a chap called with a smile.

'Yeah. I'm glad it's your problem, not mine,' I returned with a smirk.

It was good natured frustration on their part and resigned boredom on mine. I took the book out again and continued.

The flight took off, and I went for a pee. When I got back, the area was filling up again, but this time all I could hear was British accents, and I suddenly felt alien in their presence. My seat was gone, so I took another further away and was soon surrounded.

Surrounded by hot girls!

Yes, by pure chance, lots of twenty-something girlfriends were taking all the seats around me. There were some Spanish and Italians in there, but mainly American. This was better. I tried not to look old and smelly. It was impossible in my rags, but I stuck it out.

We all sat there for a long time as the place filled up. Eventually, they were running late, and people finally started boarding, slowly. We (the girls and me) all remained seated, even after they'd called us up. When the queue was down to the last few people, we all decamped and filed on board.

Back in steerage, I was at the end of a three seater, middle block, sitting next to a live wire called Charlotte. She was fabulous company and laughed at all my jokes, which was nice. We got on like a house on fire, even to the point of us taking the piss out of each other (a thing that usually takes a while to be acceptable). She even punched me on the arm at one point. It was great to have such good company on such a tedious part of the journey home, and Charlotte said, 'I'm so glad I sat next to you on the plane, you know? You never know who it might be; but you're great.' (I repeated the compliment to her later in the journey, once I had got to know her better.)

We looked out for each other—I gave her a sweet to stop her ears popping, she showed me how to work the inflight entertainment, I woke her for her food, she shared her blanket. We both enjoyed ourselves. She wasn't physically my type, but the personalities and the situation we found ourselves in made for good company. And as I said, she laughed at almost everything funny I said. At one point, she said that she was getting hot and then cold, so I said, 'Maybe you're going through the change?' This went down well (she punched me). By this time in the flight, we were comfortable enough with each other to say these things without fear, and as she was nowhere near that time in her life, the joke was obvious. Charlotte was a temp in Southampton (or Portsmouth), and she cleaned a couple of old blokes' houses on the side to make up her money. Her mum lived in New York and had brought her brother, his new wife (of a year), and Charlotte over to celebrate another brother's twenty-first birthday. Her recently married brother had to sleep in separate beds, because his wife couldn't share (which didn't bode well), even at their own home. He looked like one of the Weasley twins from *Harry Potter*.

I watched *Casablanca* and then *The Author* on the flight movies. Which one do you think I enjoyed the most? At the end of the flight, I got Charlotte's bags down for her (she was quite short), and she was gone. I didn't even see her in Heathrow airport later. Strangers on a plane . . .

HEATHROW
(DEATHROW)

CORNWALL
(KERNOW)

British passport control was non-existent for us citizens, and with no need to collect luggage, I was quickly back at the bus terminal, with an hour and a half in hand before my final journey. I sat with a coffee outside and smoked my American tobacco until I ran out and had to buy some more from the WH Smiths franchise in the station. The girl at the counter took my order for tobacco and offered me a chocolate bar promotion.

'No thanks. That stuff's bad for you, you know?'

She looked at my tobacco with a smile, acknowledging my joke.

'So is this stuff,' she nodded at the tobacco.

'But I can only do one bad thing at a time,' I countered with a suggestive smile.

I wandered back out for a smoke and to kill some final minutes before I needed to queue for the National Express coach.

I'd soon be home, but standing outside Heathrow airport, I had some time to ponder my journey, and inevitably, the pining to continue it was strong.

It was strange to be back, but I felt like I'd really been on an adventure. In my mind, I started thinking about all the places I could've been if someone noticed me and asked. I did look different to the other travellers—they all had suitcases or bags; I was the only one with nothing but, clearly, a world weary look. Dishevelled and suntanned, I imagined I was just back from a war reporting assignment somewhere exotic (they always choose 'exotic' when it comes to war destinations these days). Oh yes, I was a writer returning for a new assignment, and soon I'd be away again to my exciting life documenting the world. I smoked another cigarette and sat, doing my best impersonation of nonchalant wisdom. I'd seen some things that these mere mortal holiday makers could never even imagine. I was a man of the world. I think the Hemmingway film, which included quite a bit about his time in Spain's civil war, had made an impression on me. Not the extent that I wanted to be a war correspondent, but that the writer, and more importantly, the romance of the writer's life had possessed me. I found myself looking up at the sky a great deal, wishing I was up there somewhere on a flight to somewhere unknown, maybe sipping a martini in business class, still looking scruffy, which would be part of my charm. The other passengers, in their ignorance, would look down at my dress, but the hot stewardesses would be excited and fawn over me. Obviously, I would flirt, but merely to please them and would leave them feeling shallow and tardy as I left the aircraft in some far flung hell hole at the start of my next chapter.

My God, I was infatuated with myself. Or was it just the glory of the imagination? I'd got used to fending for myself again in strange situations, and I felt seventeen once again. An age when the future only held opportunities, not responsibilities. I could reinvent myself, if only I could hold an accent. All these things passed through my mind as I waited for my coach home.

When it did, I put those thoughts aside and joined the depressing queue of citizens heading home from their various holidays. The only talk was between the driver and these people. Nobody looked happy. In fact, they looked downtrodden and miserable. He checked my ticket with a nod, and I was on board.

I sat as near to the front as possible. There was a girl sitting already in a seat, and so I sat next to her. All the other double seats were occupied by one person each, and so I thought, if I've got to share, I'd rather it be with a female. What a great choice. She roundly ignored me for the whole journey and, as soon as she could, moved seat to be alone again. Nobody spoke on the coach, except for the driver to tell us times and upcoming destinations along the way. What a typical British experience. Welcome back from the world, but here we mind our own business, and we'd prefer you to do the same.

From thirty thousand feet in the air to thirty thousand feet underground in only two hours. It was after about half an hour I remembered why I wanted to leave this country. By an hour, I was already formulating my next journey.

This depression was only countered by the knowledge that soon I would be seeing my children and wife again, and that was such a buzz. I felt what I expect a bipolar person feels on a regular basis. Highs crashing into lows, ups of emotional love smashing into deep, dark lows. Just to give the story a perfect background, it started to rain heavily.

Unlike the Greyhound, there were no two-hour layovers or stops for cigarettes every two hours. When people got off the bus, the driver was quickly back to his seat and we were off again, as if he was scared of a cold backside or something. We stopped for a minute or two here and there and only slightly longer if he had to chuck somebody's suitcase off before wheel spinning away, leaving the hapless traveller in a spray of dirty rain water. In the six hours it took to get back to St. Austell, we had one stop of twenty minutes early on around Reading, and then another similar one at Plymouth only occurred because our replacement bus driver was late. There was less customer care than I'd seen in America in almost every aspect of this final leg. People were questioned without pity or respect if they deviated from a company policy. There was no room for variations of human existence. No questioning the logic of a ruling, and of course, everyone fell into line, just like they always do here.

Eventually, the passing scenery became recognisable again, and I started mentally ticking off the towns as we passed through them. At nearly six o'clock in the afternoon, we pulled into St. Austell's bus station, where I'd sat so long ago on a cool evening listening to drunken shouts and wondering what lay ahead of me. Now here I was; back in my home town, and quickly saw Julie pull in with the kids in the car waving. Somehow, I expected them to already be waiting for me, but they were right on time as I stepped down onto Cornish soil once more and into the arms of my loving family.

What Happened Next . . .

Riding the dawg and the iron horse all happened in one extended adventure, but I had to wait another two years before taking a hog down the Mississippi River and completing the triple. Obviously, there was the financial restrictions, but mainly it was because I didn't have a bike licence and had to go through that extended process of learning how to ride the damn thing. This also had a financial cost (about £600 in the end), and this too was a surprising journey for me.

I thought I'd learn to ride well away from my home turf, so that I could concentrate on the job in hand and not get distracted by locals, and at the same time, I thought it would be better to be on neutral ground, so that my skills could take me on unfamiliar roads with safety. So I bought myself a £700 Honda Shadow 125cc cruiser from a bloke at work who had just passed his test and hooked up with a bike school forty miles away.

To start with there was a half-day CBT course to complete, which involved riding around cones and emergency stopping and then out onto the highways looking for adventure . . . (but mainly road signs).

Easily completed, I moved on to riding the school's big boy bikes (650cc Bandits), scaring the shit out of other road users and myself at times, all the while putting the road miles in on the Shadow back at home. Through rain and hail, I bravely rode my mini cruiser to and from work each day, went out at weekends when the rest of the world was asleep and practiced all the manoeuvres that I'd learnt on the 650.

I needed to take my theory test before I was allowed to apply for my two practical tests (one off-road around cones etc. and one

139

on the road). Of course, my confidence was up, being a car driver for thirty years, and of course, I fucked up my theory test by one mark. Happy days. I reapplied, paid again, and passed easily the second time, with a slightly weary, resigned look upon my chops as the official handed me the coveted confirmation slip and headed back to the bike school.

While this was all going on, my mother-in-law was dying of cancer up country, and Julie was having to spend time away from home over an extended period, taking the kids with her, to be with her mother. It was an emotional time for the family, myself included. While not being particularly close to my own, I had adopted Julie's parents and felt this loss on a massive scale. I'd already buried her father a few years back, and now we were having to go through this all again. To make matters worse, I couldn't be with her in her lowest moments. Long phone calls can't make up for the touch of your partner. Julie had to take the kids up and down the 500 miles round journey, because I worked at night and they couldn't be left at home alone, so there was the added strife for her to worry about them, their schooling, and welfare while away from home. The strain was immense for our relationship, but we clung on for dear life as the days ticked by towards the inevitable conclusion. Janet knew all about my plans and even left me money to help pay for the journey. (So this one's for you, Jan, x).

They were long, lonely forty-mile journeys to and from the bike school for me. Coming home after a long day to an empty house and having no-one to unload my thoughts on helped to batter my confidence as I dissected every moment from the days, focussing on my faults and fears. But the test days were looming, and family or not, I had to take them.

Just as Janet was passing, I took my first practical test (cones, emergency stop, and the dreaded slow motion U-turn). I completely went to pieces. The journey home in the car was dreadful. I felt sorry for myself. Sorry for my wife and for our kids. And I wiped tears from my eyes as I drove, trying to find something positive from the day. But I couldn't. She was gone. I was alone.

After the funeral, I retook the practical test and passed, fucked up the road test (because I didn't overtake a bus that pulled in to let some passengers on), retook that, and finally passed on December the 5th. I was glad to see the back of that instructor (as he probably was of me).

I promptly sold the 125cc Shadow (£1500—thank you very much!) and bought a 794cc Triumph Bonneville America so I could get used to riding the bigger bike that I had waiting for me across the ocean. I started putting road miles on the new bike and looked towards the future . . .

STAGE FOUR-THE RETURN . . .

THE HOG

Friday July 3rd 2015

New York City
("The Big Apple")

7PM in Manhattan. This has been a fuck of a long day.

It started in Cornwall at about 3PM on Thursday afternoon. In UK terms, it's midnight, but here the night is young. I shall disregard its age and go to sleep anyway. I am too old and knackered to play silly buggers after such a long journey.

Ju dropped me off at the bus station at 9.50PM and waved me away as I rode the National Express into the night. We had three driver changes along the way, but no bus changes, so I sat tight until Heathrow, and then against the bus people's suggestion of taking another coach to terminal five an hour or two later, I took the underground tube thing there in half the time, and after an initial problem with location (because they'd moved since the last time I was here in 2012), found the Wetherspoons and started to consume three pints of ale. Happy daze.

Okay. I'll tell you more tomorrow. I'm knackered now, I need sleep xx

And so disaster lurked around every corner on my first night back in New York after three years. This part of my story got off to a particularly bad start . . .

On the plane, I was sat with a Scottish couple (Cheryl and Murray), who were friendly, in their fifties, and visiting the states for the first time. He ran a business in Inverness, and she was an ex-international hockey player, or something. I liked them both, and we chatted easily. I drank thirteen free single malts. The vegan food was both excellent and first to be served.

I love British Airways. They are fabulously professional (even in steerage), and the fact that the monitors were down, and so no films were available, made little difference as the eight hours or so zipped by in comfort. I always choose BA, even if it's a little more expensive, because of the previous experiences I've had with them. They just ooze 'we know what we're doing,' whereas most other companies seem to be staffed by shop assistants who appear amazed to be flying at all. It's like BA is staffed by consultants, and all the other companies are staffed by their receptionists. And the one thing you need when travelling at 560 miles an hour, at 30,000 feet, is a little professionalism.

By the end of the flight, my phone was running out of power, so I turned it off to preserve what was left. BA didn't have any charging ports on the seats we were sat in. I don't know if this has since changed.

Got through customs easily enough after a chat about riding motorcycles across the country with the staff and then a great taxi ride into the city; a lovely chatty fellow who'd also ridden a bike from New York to Los Angeles and back (so we had much to talk about).

My luggage on this journey was similar to last time—my trusty shoulder bag but with my motorcycle helmet along for the ride (literally). And that's it. You could've hired a helmet with the bike, but as they charged ten dollars a day just for that, I thought I'd take my own. Travelling light was both sensible and less complicated, considering the means of transport involved. I prefer it like this; there's less to lose, less to have to think about, less time wasted waiting for luggage to appear, and generally it costs less. If you're going to a destination and staying there, I can understand the desire for more luggage, but for me, the journey is the thing. Travelling light also frees your mind from the theoretical baggage, leaving your mind with more capacity to experience the moment. Immersing yourself in your surroundings and becoming invisible to others helps you to bear witness. Also, you don't look like such a dick with your little suitcase trundling behind you down the sidewalk, screaming, 'Rob me! Rob me! I'm a tourist!'

> *Got to destination. Phone was dead. Shit. Couldn't get in the building, let alone the room (which Scarlett hadn't ever told me the number of anyway).*

Scarlett was my (so-called) host in New York, because in the two years since I'd last been in the city, The Hotel Carter had finally been closed down. Typical. As soon as I find the perfect place to stay, some fucker shuts it down. I'd hunted for an alternative for a while, but within my price range, Manhattan was becoming impossible. So I'd had to look for an alternative. The obvious choice was AIRBNB. I located a place to stay near to where the Carter still stood and communicated with chap over a number of months, until at the very last moment (a week or two before I left), he cancelled the deal and refunded my money, due to unforeseen circumstances. Fuck! Now everything was organised, and I had no place to stay for the first two nights of my stay in America. Frantically, I scoured AIRBNB for a replacement and found Scarlett Jin at 207 East 33rd Street.

Now, East 33rd is on the opposite side of Manhattan from where I wanted to be, but it was low enough down the island and within a similar price range, so I jumped on it. The accommodation wasn't as good (effectively, a corner of the kitchen with a curtain across it for privacy), but as I wasn't intending spending any time other than sleeping there, it didn't really matter much. The photos online looked good enough, considering that the alternative was a doorway. Theoretically, I would be sharing with someone else (but that turned out to be a lie), and we'd clearly be getting to know each other quite well with the accommodation consisting of a kitchen, a locked room to the front of the building with the only window in the 'apartment' in it, and a shower room off the kitchen. I hoped my curtain was thick.

When I stepped out of the taxi in front of 207 East 33rd, it was boiling hot sunshine that greeted me as I attempted to get my bearings. Around me were tall grey buildings with railing and steps leading upwards to glass doors. My particular building was non-descript but with a swipe card entry system that I hadn't expected.

To be honest, I'd expected mein host to be waiting to greet me, but as far as I could see into the lobby beyond, there was nobody there.

In the intervening two years since my last visit to the States, I'd also given up smoking. It was at this point I suddenly started thinking about cigarettes for some reason.

I tried a nearby bar, after asking a few people who entered and left 207 if they knew Scarlett.

It's an unusual name, so I thought someone might know her, but like many cities, people keep themselves to themselves and the people I asked seemed genuinely surprised to be even spoken to. Mind you, perhaps it had more to do with how I was dressed in the 30C heat. I didn't see many other people in black leather jackets carrying black motorcycle helmets with bleached hair and black shades on. Sweating like dogs.

The bar had a machine to charge mobiles ($2.49 for half an hour), so I had a couple of cold beers as I waited for the phone to suck power. The bar was open to the sidewalk, and even in the shade, it was very hot as I sweated.

I'd told Scarlett when my flight was expected in at JFK and when I'd be arriving so she could let me in. Now the day was drifting away into a lazy, Friday early evening, and I had been travelling without sleep for nearly twenty-four hours.

Thirteen inflight whiskies, three airport ales, two New York lagers, and now back to our man on the street;

The phone was charged a bit, but for some reason I couldn't get through to Scarlett on the number she'd given me. I sent messages to everyone explaining my predicament and nothing came back. Then the phone died again. I sent one final message to Julie pleading for her to contact Scarlett and let me in. And then nothing.

I charged the phone for a second, longer time (five dollars this time) and left it in the machine while I went around the corner of the block.

Stood outside the building for a couple of hours, hoping that she'd come down and let me in, or I'd at least see her leaving and catch her then, but to no avail. Instead, I just sweated and fretted. Then a woman crossed the street towards me and called out in a loud voice, for everyone to hear,

'Oh my! You're real!' and, 'You are SO beautiful! I thought you were a mannequin someone had left out.'

I didn't know how to deal with this statement, so I just said thank you and smiled. No-one has ever said this to me in all my life, (I was forty-eight years old at the time), and I was so chuffed my little chest puffed up like a gay winter Robin for a minute, until the memory faded and the sweat returned to trickle down my arse crack.

I decided I must find help, or at least somewhere to sleep. I went to my old haunt; Smiths Bar on the other side of town. Of course, while I'd turned my back on New York for two years, my favourite barman, Mike, had left the bar (after working there for twenty-three years) and the new people didn't have a clue as to where he was. Fuck. I went around the corner to the New York Brewing Company. Nothing. My friend, Kara, had moved onto a career in films by now, and they were too busy to help me. Hotels were fully booked or $500+ for a few nights. Hotel Carter was shut completely (since March) under new owners. Eventually, I walked around for what seemed like miles, carrying all my stuff. Tired and exhausted, I finally got a text from Scarlett, and after another taxi ride back to the East Side, I was let into the building.

Ju later said that she'd been quite unpleasant with her on the phone, being abrupt and all, 'What's it got to do with you?' 'Who ARE you?', 'Where is he?', and 'I can't wait here all this time!' All because she wouldn't answer the phone number she'd given me when I rang or reply to texts that I sent. If she'd had any sense, she'd have told me that the door to the building needed a swipe card to get in (which I obviously wouldn't have) and which number the actual flat was (so I might ask someone to knock on the door for me), however, that was by the by, because now I was in the flat.

When I got to her room on the 4th floor, she was short in stature and quick to leave. A door key, a swipe card, and a swift bloody exit. The bed collapsed on me as I lay down.

Jetlagged and knackered from walking, I fell asleep. Waking six hours later (7AM UK time), I spoke to Jess and Ju for the first time and then tried to sleep some more until New York woke at 7AM USA time. So much for Friday.

They call New York time Eastern Seaboard Time (EST—like we have GMT), so I'll try to be more professional with my references from herein (why bother now?).

So this was the 3rd of July in New York City. Yes, I kind of knew it was an important couple of days in the American calendar, and I'd sort of planned to be here when I was, but I wasn't ready for the tension and expectation, the influx of people, and the chaos that presents to the jetlagged. Looking back on those first few nightmarish hours on the ground, I can see the funny side of it now, but at the time, it was truly horrendous. I was alone and becoming more desperate as the hours ticked by; my brain crumbling in the cacophony of traffic and sunshine. I just wanted to lie down and sleep somewhere. The alcohol probably didn't help, but then it wouldn't have been a problem if all things had gone to plan. I would've been asleep in a kitchen hours ago, behind my wafer thin security curtain, on my collapsed bed.

After Scarlett had left, and before the bed had collapsed on me, I'd made a survey of the accommodation and found that there was only plastic cutlery and paper cups to drink from, no discernible food (it was all written in Japanese/Chinese, and the pictures gave you little hope of surmising what the food even was anyway), some manky coffee, and two very sharp metal paring knives (which I hid on top of the cupboard, in case my fellow resident came home late at night and decided to despatch me as I lay in the kitchen). Of course, there was no 'fellow resident,' as that was a lie Scarlett had told me so that she could keep the best room in the place locked and leave me in the window-less hole, with the broken bed, away from the view of the street below, and probably her TV and real bed.

Looking around the kitchen, I saw some junk mail and old letters stuffed beside the kettle, and it soon became clear that Scarlett was not her real name either.

I also discovered there was a window in the kitchen. It was A4 sized and, through the dirty glass, had a view of a red brick wall about two feet away. With a bit of contortion, I could tell that the window was looking into an external chimney affair of some sort that may well have been a ventilation shaft. There were other grimy windows of similar sizes dotted up and down the shaft and only the briefest of hints that daylight might be somewhere high above. It was like being halfway down a well.

[NYC–Empire State of mind]

Saturday 4th July 2015

New York City
(Independence Day) . . .

*Was awake for hours before finally giving up and getting up.
Had a shower (cold, and not through choice) and tried to clean
yesterday's sweat out of my shirt.*

*I went out for breakfast, to a local diner, a few blocks away, which
had good reviews on the net. (Murray Hill Diner, 222 Lexington
Avenue) It was as good as it was pricey. I had a stack of pancakes with
bananas and a coffee for just over ten dollars. There were too many
pancakes for me, but the free coffee refills really helped.*

Okay, lets address the elephant in the room (almost literally).
In my experience, American portion sizes are very similar to the
UK. I know that goes against all the information that you've
previously ingested, but it's the truth. What our media likes
to feed us are the extremes of life, not the mundane. In both
America and the UK, I've seen those extremes, but I would say
that generally Americans are as aware of their health as much as
anybody.

I chose the pancakes, because I knew I'd never finish them,
but at the same time, I wanted to taste an authentic American
breakfast. A hell of a lot of Americans don't eat pancakes for
breakfast, and I'm not really a breakfast sort of guy anyway.
Black coffee and a cigarette or two has generally been my
wake-up call of choice throughout my life, but here I was in
New York City on the fourth of July, and some things just have
to be done.

I felt like a stuffed pig as I waddled back to the apartment.

I then tried to figure out the phone system here. '+1' doesn't actually mean '+' and '1,' so why don't all numbers just have an extra '1' at the start? Bloody stupid, if you ask me.

I'd emailed Gjoni over the last two years, getting to know him and his family, and although he had also left New York (this time for Portland), he was coming back to meet me in the city once again. His wife and daughters still lived here, but he had to leave to find other work when the Russian restaurant closed. (He emailed me at the time to tell me it was up for sale for $12 million.) We'd exchanged phone numbers and agreed to meet up today for a get-together over beers.

I couldn't get a reply from Gjoni, so I went out walking the streets of my favourite city, every so often catching a glimpse of the Empire State building between other skyscrapers as I crossed avenues, generally heading to the centre of town. I picked up some postcards and stamps along the way, with less hassle than last time(!) and ended up at a bar called Mr.Biggs Bar and Grill on 43rd and 10th.

They only had forty-eight draft beers on tap, but I thought I'd give them a chance and pulled up a barstool in the nearly empty saloon. Saturday afternoon drinking is not really an American thing. They call it 'day drinking' (which I quite like), but it's not an activity that many seem to indulge in. That's fine. I don't like crowds.

I sat at the bar and chatted to the staff as they went about their business. There was a nice barmaid, who's name I've completely forgotten, and she helped me with selecting each new beer. I'd finally got through to Gjoni on the phone, and by the time he turned up, I was on my sixth or seventh pint. Quickly, he tried to get me to eat something, but I was having none of it and continued to drink as he munched away on something fried from the bar. We chatted like old friends, and both remarked on how each of us had changed appearance in just a few years. After getting him to have a drink with me, and noticing the bar was beginning to fill up, he suggested we go somewhere else.

We took a taxi to Ground Zero, where the Twin Towers used to stand, to see the monument with all the dead people's names on it. It was a poignant moment for me, looking at all the names and picking out the Cornish ones, but Gjoni didn't seem to be affected

and so patiently waited for me to mooch around and finally buy a
souvenir programme for ten dollars in the beautiful sunshine. I was
choked up and couldn't even take a proper photograph.

So then we went on to another bar somewhere, and that's
where it starts to get hazy.

I remember it was a bit of a trek south and east from Ground
Zero and that it was a walk-down basement bar. The people seemed
to know Gjoni, and I was introduced as his friend. We had a few
more drinks and then, nothing.

So I'll let Gjoni explain what happened:

Nothing happened, Alex! You behaved fine to the end as
long as we were together! Of course you had a few beers,
and alcohol was affecting your balance and concentration
near the end! I wanted to get you a cab, to get you at the
hotel room but you insisted you wanted to walk there on your
own. Since I judged you could make it there, even though the
balance became apparent. After that I do not know how you
made it there, but you were not falling, and I thought a little
walking would help.

You were fine and generous with the bartenders, and
you did not abuse the language. So nothing really serious
happened. Personally I eat when I drink, and the food softens
the effect of alcohol. That's why I bought a few appetizers,
but you insisted beer means beer, and that is the English
way and did not eat. I ate some, and the young bartender girl,
who appeared hungry, helped with the rest.

We went to a bar in a basement with the suggestion of
a fellow Hispanic customer who came next to us randomly,
and was claiming he owned two bars and he gave us the
address of one. There we changed from beer to hard liquor;
I don't remember what it was, but we both had some and
we had it quickly! My head was becoming heavy, and you
were having mild balance and concentration issues. Had we
stayed with beer only would have been much better! So that
was it! The whole thing was enjoyable.

. . . which explains why we ended up in that particular bar. My
lack of balance appears to worry Gjoni, but I insist on walking off
into the night, apparently. Like a pissed version of Captain Oates.

Next thing I know, I'm in a cab. I don't know how I got here,
don't know where we're going or what has happened. I've literally

*come to in a cab as if waking up. I check my pockets and I'm broke.
That's not good. Quickly I tell the driver all I have is four dollars.
Obviously he's angry, and after I've placated him, explained things,
offered my watch as payment (he takes a look at it and hands it
back in disgust!), and persuaded him not to take me to the cops, he
gives me his address and makes me promise to send him the twenty
dollars he wants. Then he throws me out of the cab, and I start
walking.*

*Drunk at night on foot. New York City. Do-able if it wasn't the
fourth of July and every other road was blocked off by the police. I
must've walked for a couple of hours before I got home. Zigzagging
due to closed roads and alcohol, trying to keep focussed on where I
was heading, while everyone I met headed away from me towards
the firework display on the West Sde of the island.*

*I'd lost my postcards and my Twin Towers souvenir booklet
(well, I chucked it actually, because I was so frustrated trying to get
back), and worst of all, the pass key for the building.*

*Luckily, people were going in, so I followed them. And even
more luckily, I hadn't lost my room key. I think the pass key must
have come out with my four dollars in the cab, so it's on his backseat
I guess. Wherever that is.*

*Not a good day. I don't know what happened to Gjoni. The
fireworks were quite nice though (as much of them as I saw), and
I'm amazed I didn't lose my phone.*

Could've been worse . . .

Earlier in the day, I'd taken a couple of photos of cops loitering
on the street corner, and they hadn't looked very friendly when
they saw what I was doing, so I imagine I would've been in a whole
lot of trouble if they'd found me drunk on the streets later. I mean,
generally I'm a quiet drunk; a little stumbly, a little staggerly, but
generally no bother to anyone. However, on this particular day of
the year in this particular location, I think the New York Police
Department would have taken great pleasure in detaining me.
Thankfully they were all tied up with crowd control.

So I stumbled up the stairs into the 'apartment' and collapsed
once more on to my already collapsed bed. For some reason, in the
time I'd been out of the building, all the corridors and stairs, of the
entire building, had been coated in a fine white dust, as if someone
had let off fire extinguishers or something. Either that, or I'd been
gone a lot longer than I thought, and the dust had really taken hold.

Sunday 5th July 2015

New York City (NY)
("The Empire State")

Chicago (IL)
(. . . Try and Guess This One)

Woke up a few times after texting Julie about my disastrous day. Finally got up and had a shower at around 6.30AM.

The people in this building are fucking arseholes. All through the night they shout at each other as they bang doors and stamp around. It's the worst, noisiest place I've ever tried to sleep in (and I've fallen asleep on railway stations in both the UK and France!). This is their home for fucks sake, what is the matter with them?

My train to Chicago left at 3PM, but without my building key, I didn't feel much like doing any last minute sightseeing. I'd spent over $200 on beer yesterday, and I was still confused about how the events of the previous day had unfolded. I'd never woken up in a taxi before; that was new. I hadn't blacked out on booze for nearly thirty years. As I sat in the corner of the kitchen, I wondered if someone had slipped me a micky finn and rolled me when I was out. I had no money, but my phone was still with me. I checked my body for bruising, but I appeared to be unscathed. It was all a strange mystery to me on that sunny Sunday morning in New York City.

Not looking forward to telling Scarlett I've lost her pass key. I don't know when I'm expected to vacate, but I imagine it's before

twelve noon. I guess I'll head for Penn Station then. It's quite a
confusing crap hole apparently.

As was the inside of my brain that morning.

> *There's no telly in this room. There's no windows that show*
> *anything but a brick wall. It's like a prison cell. What an auspicious*
> *start to this trip.*

And so I sat, my meagre belongings packed in seconds and a
bitter black coffee in a polystyrene cup slowly going cold. I read
my few guide books about cities I was intending to visit along the
Mississippi, and slowly the hours drifted by. Sundays always seem to
have extra-long hours, especially when you're waiting for something.

I started to text Scarlett about the pass key, but somewhat
predictably, she didn't reply to any of them. At midday, I rang her
number, but she wouldn't answer her phone (as soon as I'd rung off,
she suddenly answered my texts). After a few more texts and she
understood that the swipe key was missing, she said that I should
leave the apartment key on the table with twenty-five dollars to
cover the cost of a new swipe key. I thought about that. The flat
would be unlocked. The money would be on the table. What's to
stop someone just walking in and nicking the money? (Or someone
later claiming that they had?) I didn't like the idea at all and took
her other option of leaving the dispute up to AIRBNB. I would
have handed the money over to her in person with the flat key, if
she could have been bothered to return to the flat, but for some
reason, she didn't want any physical interaction. I felt bad, but she
had been incredibly unwelcoming to me since I'd first got there and
it felt very much like she was actively trying to do the exact opposite
of being a host (which is one of the things that AIRBNB promote
as their significant difference to your usual rental experiences).

Anyway, I decided that it felt like I was being set up for
something, so cautiously I left the building with the door to room
4B unlocked, but no cash left inside, and hoped for the best.

Her review on the AIRBNB website . . . and my reply:

> Scarlett Jin
> 1) on check-in day I waited him in home for the whole
> afternoon and could not reach him until his wife called me

from England to let me open the door for him, but I still didn't see him after the phone call. I had to refill my phone to use the international roaming and text him at 80 cents per message. 2) On check-out day he said he lost the key card and promised that he would pay me back, so I request extra fee through AIRBNB, but it's been two weeks and haven't heard back from him at all. 3) bathtub was stuck with hair.

And my response
3) As there is no BATHTUB in the flat, I find it hard to imagine how I could personally leave any hair in it! I stayed for two unfortunate nights. I do not have alopecia (she is clearly insane) 2) I have been travelling for two weeks and have only just returned from the USA. I did NOT promise to pay her back for losing her key card (my wallet, containing the card & many other credit card, was stolen whilst I was there). She has no communication skills and never answered a single phone call, so I was unable to tell her what had happened. In fact she never replied to a single e-mail that I sent her before the stay over a period of six months either. & 1) She never bothered to tell me that her building contained many flats and which one I was staying in, so I was stuck out on the street in the boiling sunshine for two hours trying to get her to answer a phone call. To the point my phone battery died and I had to go around the corner to a pub and get it charged ($2.49) and call my wife back in the UK to get her to call this host for me. Scarlett was very rude to my wife on the phone, and when I finally did get into the building, she stomped off within a minute and I never saw or heard from her again however much I tried to contact her. Frankly she is dire. She shouldn't be allowed to host AIRBNB.

Now I know what you're thinking; and yes, I did embellish the truth a little in my reply, but she claimed I blocked up her non-existent bath with clods of my hair! It's a pretty impressive claim, as I was only there for two nights. On that basis, I should've been bald before I got to Chicago. I was insulted by her review (but not surprised), and after reading other reviews by her guests, I realised that I was not alone. She tried to raise a claim with AIRBNB against me, but they came down in my favour and, in fact, gave me a fifty-dollar voucher to apologise for my unpleasant experience (which I've never used). In my opinion, she didn't deserve any sympathy after the way she spoke to Julie on that first night, but her behaviour from that point on was so bizarre that I stopped using normal rules of morality to understand her and packed the memory of her away in a filing cabinet marked, 'Nuts.'

So I guess you want to know a bit about New York City from someone who's been there three or four times? Well here's a thumbnail sketch covering a few things: it's not as busy as you'd expect, it's not as dirty as London, there's not really that much traffic (most of which seems to be taxis), the pavements/sidewalks are wide, flat, and generally gum-free, pedestrians that aren't tourists are generally not as rude as those in London, and overall, when the sun shines, there's really no better place to be. It reeks of diversity in culture, the steam does actually rise up from manholes in the winter, and if you've got a touch of ADD, you'll love the grid system. It's not as cheap as you'd hope (about the same as London prices generally), tipping is pretty much compulsory regardless of quality of service provided, and when they say, 'Have a nice day' you can't hear any sarcasm. Obviously, there are still dirty streets and shitty people (it's a busy city), but overall the feeling is of safety and enthusiasm. You can hear the locals in conversation, if you spend a little time keeping your mouth shut, and pick up snippets of their true lives. Or you can treat it all like a theme park with the locals as exhibits and stand slack-jawed at the movie you've stepped into. You could stuff food at every opportunity, photograph everything, and come away with no more actual knowledge than you would've had from your computer back at home. My advice? Take as few photos as you can, listen as much as you can, and keep your opinions to yourself.

You could spend a month in the city and still have only the vaguest of impressions of what it's like to live in Manhattan, but that's the same with anywhere I guess. Anywhere except St. Austell. A few hours there pretty much covers everything you'll ever need to know. What I'm saying is that New York City is nothing like St. Austell in the same way that chocolate cake is nothing like dog shit. Well I'm hoping it isn't anyway, otherwise that's a lot of free cake I've stepped in over the years.

And so ends the advert for New York City. Visit it if you want, it won't let you down (St. Austell, on the other hand . . .).

Back to the story: Outside the building, the Sunday sun was up high, and the weekend life of a city was humming. There's no rush on a Sunday, the weekend is nearly over and everyone is just wandering around, pottering about, and tying up loose ends before the Monday morning alarm bell screams in your ear. The party nights on Friday and Saturday are done, the celebration is over, so the day is spent reflecting on what we did and what will come. The streets are quieter than usual, even at noon, and so I had to walk a while to find a cab.

At Penn Station, in the underground city, it was busy. Thousands of people thronged through the thoroughfare. Police and soldiers mingled with customers and assorted nutters with automatic weapons ready to make a name for themselves. Potential terrorists bought candy bars and asked their parents for bottles of Coke, and all was well in the world.

I made my way down deeper (on down) into the bowels of this mausoleum of mayhem and eventually found a seat near to where my train would be leaving from. I had three hours to kill. People (remember to take a breath between those two words please) watching is a favourite pastime of mine, and in such a place, the advantage is that after a while, a whole new batch arrive to take the place of those that you have judged or created backstories for. The conveyor belt continues, and you start all over again. If it gets too much for you, whip out a book and start reading it in public—that'll surprise most people and create an image of intellectual superiority that is never the tipping point for a mob to turn upon a bystander and pummel him into the ground shouting, 'Kill the reader, kill the reader.' Best to take out a mobile phone and stare at it. I took out mine, but it's very hard to out-stare an iPhone (they haven't got any eyes; they can't blink. They always win. It's not fair. Bloody Steve Nobs). I put my phone away and continue being intellectual in public. Surprisingly, I'm not burnt at the stake for being a witch by the donut consuming masses surrounding me, and the hours slowly tick by.

I hadn't eaten since Saturday's pancake breakfast, but it was thirst that was really getting to me. By the time we were all boarded onto the number 49 train to Chicago Union Station, it'd been over four hours since I'd drank anything, and I was really starting to suffer. I asked a ticket bloke on board when I could get some water, and he said in about five minutes, so I left my stuff and walked the length of the train to the café section (which was shut) and waited in the non-air conditioned joint part between carriages. Half an hour later, with me now dripping with sweat, a woman came out

*from the café and, after asking me to move, proceeded to phone
message the whole train about what was available in the café that
she was in charge of. After about five minutes of this, she let me into
the café area. I waited. She collected some till receipts. I waited. A
queue started to form. I waited. She washed her hands. I waited.
Eventually, as if she hadn't noticed me before that second, she asked
what I wanted. I was tempted to say, 'Nothing,' but my thirst got
the better of me and so I actually said, 'Two bottles of water, two
cans of Pepsi, a bottle of orange juice, and two plastic beakers of ice,
please'... (just over eleven dollars and I didn't leave a bloody tip).*

She was an utter twat with absolutely no people skills and the
polar opposite of my last Amtrak experience. Hopefully she is the
exception that proves the rule when it comes to the trains, because
at every other opportunity, I found Amtrak employees to be more
than helpful and friendly. I hope she scalds her hand on a hot kettle.

I was concerned that my possessions might've been either nicked
or blown up in a controlled explosion in my absence. If I'd known
it was going to take so long, I would've said something to a fellow
passenger. Wandering back through the train, I found, to my relief,
that I was still on an Amtrak train zipping through the northern
New York state and hadn't yet been whisked through a wormhole
back to a crappy Virgin train crawling towards Doncaster. The
fleeting views of the city were hard to avoid through the windows,
and keeping focussed on not spilling my drinks as I walked was
quite a skill. But when I got back, nothing had gone, and so I sat
and cooled myself through liquid and ice. Eighteen hours and five
minutes to kill.

Ugh, I seem to be the one all the conductors wanted to talk to,
and I even had to spell my name out to one buffoon. It seems that
she was not the exception to the rule. My mood began to darken
along with the daylight after I offered a girl sitting alongside me,
one of my Pepsis only to have her turn it down. I shouldn't have
bothered, but I thought a little friendliness would balance things
out in the universe.

*As we travelled through some beautiful landscape (the Great
Lakes of the Canadian border are amazing), the train slowly filled
up until all the seats were taken. I had to share with a sporty mum
who had two young daughters in nearby seats. They reminded me*

of Jess so much it hurt, and I could hardly bring myself to talk to the woman.

Eighteen hours on a train, and I didn't get out of my seat again. The sporty woman had so much stuff (compared to my measly shoulder bag and helmet), I felt bad about having to push past it all to get out of the seat. So I didn't eat, go to the loo, get any more to drink, or even sleep much (about an hour in total, I think), due to the noise and seat position. I was a prisoner of Sue Barker.

A window seat is normally ideal on a train, but less so on a night journey. As our journey progressed, my view became less vivacious on one side and more vacuous on the other.

Monday 6th July 2015

CHICAGO, (IL)
("THE WINDY CITY"), ("THE PRAIRIE STATE")

TIPTON, IOWA (IA)
(. . . WAIT FOR IT)

Sunday night turned into Monday morning, and as the light came into the skies, we pulled into Chicago Union Station bang on time as always. It never ceases to amaze me how much shit we put up with in the UK when it comes to travel and service; it's almost as if we're brought up to expect the worst and then revel in our misery like some Stockhausen victim support group.

No fault of Amtrak, but I was truly knackered as I stumbled up out onto the street that morning. I was instantly hit by the bustle of the city as people around me hurried to the start of their working week, weaving between each other on the sidewalk at different speeds and directions, like ants on an unexplained mission.

I dived into the second available taxi, after some Korean git just pushed past me into the first one, and took a long ride out to the Eagle Riders place (forty-five bucks plus tip). My driver was a black dude, about the same age as me, and we had a great conversation as he battled with the traffic surrounding us. Families, kids, politics, and bikes; they all were debated and agreed upon. I was sad to get out of the old Ford when he pulled up some half an hour later outside the dealership on Joliet Road. The sun was up, and the heat was on.

I was due to pick up the bike at noon, and it was ten, so I expected to have a couple of hours to relax and what have you, but they got me to sign a few things, showed me the bike, and I was away in less than an hour. I'm sure that I signed to say I didn't have supplementary insurance with them, whereas in retrospect, my own bill shows that I did (at a cost of over £200). Their records will show somewhere that I did, but I was so knackered after the journey from New York that I didn't really know what was going on.

[1800cc of raw power and leather tassels]

Before you knew it, I was pootling around the car park on a massive 1800cc Indian Vintage Chief worth $30,000, trying to get a feel for this enormous bike. Typically, at one point I came to a junction, misjudged my balance, and dropped the bike on its side. It was lucky I got my leg out in time, because I couldn't lift it back up. Oh shit. A few people drove slowly around me, until one nice bloke stopped and asked if he could help. Together we managed to get the bike back upright, and I asked him if he thought one man could do

it alone, to which he replied shaking his head. I thanked him, and
he was on his way. I hoped the people who had just signed the bike
over to me thirty yards away hadn't noticed and proceeded to drive
around the car park trying to figure out the road markings, which
side I should be on, and not dropping the fucking bike again.

Eventually, I had to bite the bullet and ride on the road.

Then I got miserably lost. Thirteen miles of aimless driving, sweat pouring off my face inside my helmet, I finally pulled into a filing station and begged for some map advice. It turned out I was miles away from where I thought I was and heading in completely the wrong direction. After some useful advice from all the staff, I was soon on the right road (Interstate 55 South, then Interstate 80 East).

The bike chugged along much better at 60 to 70 mph than at slower speeds, but I was more than conscious of the speed limits and let the locals over take as I got used to driving on the wrong side of the road and being both over and under taken (sometimes at the same time).

The bike that I had chosen to rent was almost brand new (600 miles on the clock), blood red, with tan leather seat and saddle bags. A bit of cream piping on the tank and other sundry places, lots of chrome, white wall tyres, a keyless start (exciting stuff for us mere mortals), and yes, there were tassels. Okay, let's just talk about the tassels. Now some people thought they looked a bit feminine, some thought they gave off a bit of a 'showman' image. I, personally, didn't think too much about them for the first few days, but by day four, I too had taken against my leather haircut. Of course, I was stuck with them by then and had no choice, but I won't make the same mistake again. It's a matter of taste, and yours may differ, but to me back in the UK booking the bike, it looked the most custom-like of the selection and was one of the few without a fairing around the handlebars, which I was definitely NOT going to have. The choices were limited, and I think I chose the least likely bike that I would ever ride in the UK for a good reason. The tassels were unfortunate, but overall I really liked the look of the bike. The only real alternative at the time was a Harley-Davidson, and I think I decided on the Indian because I couldn't ever see myself on one back home. However, the whole bike did not scream 'poverty,' which would prove to be a slight problem later on.

Back on the road, the sun still boiling my sleep deprived brain, and the short journey to Tipton in Iowa, where I was destined to stay that night, was now turning into a much longer proposition, due to my poor map reading skills. It now turned out that I had two hundred miles ahead of me. I was in no position to do anything but attempt it.

Putting fuel into the bike became the next challenge, because the pumps are all self-service and none recognise my debit card. Brilliant. I have to go into the shop and ask for ten dollars to be credited to my pump number, give them the cash, and then go back out and use the pump until ten dollars is used. Theoretically, if you don't use all the ten, you can go back in and ask for the change, but I never did. The bike takes twenty dollars to fill the tank and will officially do 180 miles on a full tank. There is a fuel gauge, but no reserve tank, so at a hundred miles you start to think about topping up. I imagine running out of fuel would not be a pleasant experience.

So between two and four lanes of traffic, all belting down the Interstate, eating up the miles, when the heavens open and I am quite suddenly drenched to my pants. I can't see a goddam thing and realise I don't know this bike's ability to deal with these conditions (and I certainly doubt mine). The visibility becomes zero, and I do something I would never do back home; I pull in under a flyover, put my hazard lights on, and wait it out.

The rest of the drivers race down the road to oblivion with no discernible slowing of their speed. Most don't even put their lights on, let alone indicate when they change lanes. You literally cannot see through this rain for more than a car's length, and these nutters are doing no less than seventy, some much more. It is insane. The water on the road is literally an inch deep, and as every car passes me, a six foot wave washes over my left hand side. All the time I'm expecting to be rear ended, even though I'm on what we would call the hard shoulder, I'm practically invisible. This monsoon happens TWICE to me in 200 miles. My first 200 bloody miles.

I am knackered. (I think I mentioned this.) I am scared, I am wetter than fish piss, but I'm stuck in a bit of corner here. Driving back out onto that Interstate was probably the most frightening thing I ever had to do. But when the rain starts to calm down and when I can see three cars ahead, I pull out.

Eventually the rain stops, out comes the sun again, and I steam along the Interstate, evaporating amongst the pick-ups. Americans love a pick-up truck. They fucking love a pick-up. Always spotless, almost always a double cab, and rarely doing less than a hundred miles an hour (or so it seemed to me in my cloud of steam).

At my second fuel stop, I call Kris (who's letting me AIRBNB at her place in Tipton) and saw my phone was nearly dead. Not again. Without that, I was truly screwed. It held all my contacts and, more importantly, my maps. I warned her that I might be a little late and then headed back out onto the Interstate straight into my second monsoon of the day.

Just needed a bit more tension...

After what seemed like hours, I finally saw a signpost for Tipton, and I raised a fist in jubilation (the other drivers must have thought I was mad). Heading off that Interstate was the best thing that had happened to me that day.

The road was straight as an arrow, and the land was flat and unremarkable. You quickly get used to not seeing trees or hedges in this Northern state. Nothing seems to want to interrupt the horizon. There doesn't appear to be any crops growing or cattle grazing, just rough scrubland as far as the eye can see in all directions. It's the closest thing to a seascape on land. A road sign of any description is a welcome break from the desolation, and I hear myself saying the words to whatever the sign is advertising as I pass. The road is deserted; in ten miles a single car passes in the other direction. I can see it for five minutes before our paths cross ,and then I'm alone again.

Finally, I come to the outskirts of Tipton. It claims to be a city, but it only has 3,000 residents. I'm due to stay just the one night with Kris, but I've decided along the road into town to see if I can stay an extra night to recover. Luckily, she is fine about it, and I pay the extra sixty-five dollars in cash. I was in no state to travel any further. Having pulled the bike onto her drive, she shows me around the house and tells me that I have the house to myself, because she lives somewhere else in town, and then leaves me to it. The house, 'Spear House & Barn Bed & Breakfast' on East 9th Street, is amazing. A massive, gothic, Victorian wooden building, which the owners have done up to such a high standard that it feels like you're in a museum. It would work really well as a location for a horror movie, but I try to push that to the back of my mind.

It was seven in the evening when I finally showered and changed into clean clothes. I wandered around the house a little and decided to not go out that evening.

I still wasn't hungry, so I had a glass of tap water and went off to bed. So tired. Such a nice bed. Luxury.

[Norman Bates—my second AIRBNB of the trip]

Tuesday 7th July 2015

TIPTON, IOWA
("THE HAWKEYE STATE")

With the ceiling fan on all night, I didn't sweat at all, which made a nice change. A great night's sleep and a fresh sunny day dawning in the quiet suburban street the house was set on.

> *Still don't feel hungry at seven in the morning; not sure what to do with myself. I think my blood clot thing has occurred again, but this time in my other leg. It's just as painful' and the vein is all extended. I shall seek out a chemist, get some aspirin' and hopefully some pain relief gel of some kind.*

I'd had a blood clot in my left leg at Christmas and so remembered the symptoms quite easily (bulging vein, painful to touch, right on the side of my knee joint). The consequences could be dangerous, but my choices were slim, so I decided to soldier on and cross my fingers that things wouldn't get worse. I couldn't stop my brain from ruining the party though.

> *This and the bike insurance issue is stressing me out. Oh, and the taxi driver from Chicago telling me that down south, they'll steal my bike if I leave it unattended. Great—apparently I'm liable for $1,000 if that happens. Sigh.*
>
> *No Internet in the house and only a poor phone reception. I think I'll head into town on foot later and see if there's a chemist (or 'pharmacist,' as they say here).*

So I go outside to find a large branch from a tree has fallen onto the bike overnight.

It had caused only minor cosmetic damage, landing across the handlebars and the fuel tank, but still. WTF?

[The hog after being attacked by the local trees]

I am clearly doomed.

After clearing the debris and checking the damage, I walked into town with a spring in my step. At this rate I'd be shot before my blood clot could kill me, thus saving me money on aspirin.

Its wasn't too far (about seven blocks, as the Americans would say), and although I passed no-one else on the sidewalk, I enjoyed looking in at the houses and the odd wooden chapel that lined the streets. Tipton appears to be a quiet town (city), so fuck knows what they do to pay the bills—there's nothing but miles of fields surrounding the place as far as I could see. But however they do get their money, they don't like walking much, and so after a twenty minute wander, I came to the main shopping area, noticed the supermarket, and found a homely 'mom & pop' diner to get some traditional US of A breakfast victuals. Oh yes, I was getting deep into the American dream now, ordering 'biscuits and gravy' for my first food in a couple of days.

Biscuits and gravy turned out to be a large bowl containing some sort of herby dumplings/scones covered in a white fishy sauce, served with hometown charm and a large black coffee. It was just what I needed and set me up for recovery on this sunny morning.

While I was there, I got directions to the local pharmacy and post office and watched as a load of old bikers turned up outside on mint condition Harleys. It was all grey hair and shiny paintwork that reeked of retired bankers to me, and unsurprisingly, we didn't communicate, even though I was the only person wearing a biker's jacket amongst the twenty or so of us. If the Indian was parked outside, they might have commented I guess, but probably not. It was a rich boys' jolly from what I could see, and I don't think they would have looked favourably on my branch of motorcycling. But who knows?

After picking up some pain relief gel, aspirins, and postcards from the pharmacy ('Picturesque pancreas of Iowa,' 'Views of varicose veins,' and 'Wish you were hearing-aids'), I headed off to the post office for the stamps. ('Stamps AND postcards in the same shop?—Are you some sort of communist, boy?') It was here that somebody finally said how much they liked my accent. (Yay!)

> *This is a really lovely town; quiet, well maintained, and lots of social activities (judging from the leaflets). They have a wonderful old style cinema that looked like something out of* Back to the Future. *In fact, now that I think about it, the whole place looks like the film set. I'll keep my eyes out for any Deloreans as I cross the deserted streets.*
>
> *I'm staying tonight, so I might eat at the diner again (they have an impressive menu), or I might try and find the Mexican restaurant that Kris mentioned yesterday.*

I'm not sure that a Mexican restaurant in a small town in Iowa will be as authentic as further down south in my journey. This is about as far north as I've ever been in America, and being from Cornwall, my knowledge of pasties and geography tells me to eat local food, not local versions of other people's cuisine. (I'm also a fan of *The League of Gentlemen*, so . . .)

> *Hopefully, I'll be able to talk to Jess, Sam, and Ju later if the signal on the phone holds out. It's so rubbish here; cutting out and*

only two bars in certain areas of my bedroom, if you're lucky. It's like being at a music festival. I checked for a signal in the diner, and it was even worse. How do people around here communicate with the outside world?

Tomorrow is going to be a tricky ride; I need to find a single address in St. Louis city (a REAL city. Tipton, I'm looking at you), when I don't have a city map or, inevitably, any phone signal to help guide me. This may not end well . . .

Wednesday 8th July 2015

Tipton Iowa (IA)

Hannibal, Missouri (MO)

("THE SHOW-ME STATE")

The day dawned bright and dry. The house creaking all around me as the wood warmed in the sunshine. The bike remained undamaged by further attacks from nearby flora and fauna, and the skies were cloud free and that deep blue that reminds you of David Hockney paintings.

I gathered my things together and ate my breakfast in the empty, old house, contemplating the journey ahead.

Loneliness for the solo traveller is an issue that is dealt with in many different ways. Some find the time therapeutic and an opportunity to focus on one's true self, the 'self' we bury under the baggage we accumulate throughout our lives. Becoming aware of ourselves once again is like meeting an old friend unexpectedly. The distractions of company can make us blind to life.

For others, it's the main reason that they won't travel alone. Perhaps they fear the person they might discover after all these years.

Fear and loneliness go hand in hand for solo travellers, but the open minded don't shun these feelings, because they understand that the colours of a rainbow are more beautiful than the clouds they appear from. Happiness has no value without sadness, and so we embrace the loneliness, knowing that it will heighten the times we banish it with friends old and new.

(I know that sounds a bit wanky, but it's how I want to feel—so get over it!)

When you travel alone you become self-sufficient, and although it'd be nice to share some experiences with a friend, their company would fundamentally change the experience itself.

I'm not against travelling with people and sharing experiences, don't get me wrong, but the solo journey shouldn't be feared. The benefits easily out-weigh the supposed negatives, most of which are purely in your mind and are removed as you gain experience and confidence in your ability to deal with life.

But this isn't a self-help book, so let's get back to the journey and stop self-analysing our ability to cope with shit.

So I cancelled my St. Louis AIRBNB, because it was going to be too far for me and my painful leg, and set off early to get a crack at the day. I'll find somewhere along the way to crash out. Having looked around a bit, I think I'll head for Hannibal in Missouri, on the banks of the Mississippi, mainly because Mark Twain was born there and his house is open to the public as a museum.

Riding out of Tipton on the straight road back to the highway took a while in the morning sunshine, but I felt good, and the bike seemed unaffected by the tree attack the other day. As always, the first thought is fuel and I picked up a full tank before heading across country on the minor roads that would take me down to the Mississippi. Mostly these were deserted, without marker lines to remind me which side I should be on. It was only oncoming vehicles that gave me a clue. The landscape was bleak, but occasionally a tree or bush would appear, and of course, the road wound its way this way and that, so you soon began to lose a sense of direction. Signposts, you say? No, that would make life too easy. So check the phone satnav? No again; these roads are too small to be mapped. And are those black clouds I see ahead of me, by any chance?

It started out fine, but as I rode the weather changed until, in the middle of nowhere, the heavens opened and it started to pour down on me once again. I couldn't hide. I was soaked through to my skin for three long, cold hours until I finally gave up and stopped in Hannibal, some 180 miles away from where I had started. It was as far as I could physically go.

In a surprise move by me, I accidently drove through Hannibal on some sort of bypass and was heading away from my sanctuary, to my despair, when I spied The Hannibal Inn, a roadside motel of no discernible beauty at 4141 Market Street, just next to the highway. I pulled in, parked out front, and sploshed into the reception holding my helmet in one hand and my bag in the other. I left a trail of dripping water wherever I went and headed up to my room in a sodden and sorry state.

The two story building was centred around an indoor swimming pool and had a sort of holiday camp/sport hall feel to it. I'm not sure what sort of people would choose to stay here, but I don't think I would get on with them. When I arrived around eleven in the morning it was pretty much deserted, with just a friendly old janitor trying to catch the water leaking through the roof.

It was a quiet, empty collection of rooms around a pool, but as the evening has gone on, more and more noise has occurred from screaming, echoing punters outside my room and around the pool. It's like trying to go to sleep in a fully functioning sports centre.

My leg has been raised for about six hours, but it still hurts when I stand up—this is not a good sign. I've started to consider going home early and cancelling the whole journey. And of course, the thought of what pressurised air flights might do to my blood clot has left me unsure what to do.

The first thing I did do, when I got in the room, was to turn on all the air conditioning to its highest settings and strip off my wet clothes (after pulling the curtains). I took my boots off and literally poured half a cup of rainwater out of each of them, placed them on top of the air-con unit, and draped my other wet clothes around the room. It soon became so humid in the room that I nearly passed out, but there was nothing I could do anyway, so lay on the bed and watched the telly.

Its 9PM now, and the families are really enjoying the fucking pool. I'm sure my kids would enjoy the pool too, but I'm not here with them, so I just hate everyone down there regardless.

The janitor, Charles, (an old bearded gentleman—think Scooby Doo), told me where to buy some food and beer. He has an aunt in England, but he can't remember where; 'I seen her the other year, but I can't remember where she lives.'

[The bat phone in Hannibal]

He told me where I could get something to drink nearby, and he was a nice fella, but I got the feeling he was looked down on by the other workers who saw us talking. I liked him instantly. (In fact I liked him so much, I sent him a postcard when I got home. I'd love to know what his work thought of that when it turned up.) I went next door to an insanely well stocked filling station and picked up something to eat and drink. The drink was a large can of 'Oculto' (6%—blue agave infused beer aged on tequila barrel staves), an even larger can of 'Mango-rita' (8%—Bud Lite lime margarita made with mango), and a small bottle of Jim Beam (40% and a nod to my old Amtrak buddy, Bill Cousins).

The food consisted of a tube of Pringles (obviously) and a packet of Uncle Ray's chilli chips (religious crisps, no less). The Uncle Rays were cheap ($1) and excellently spicy, but then I noticed the writing on the back of the packet. Oh lordy.

On the other side from where all the usual guff about ingredients was, there was a story about skinny dipping, which was completely irrelevant to the crisps. Didn't even mention food. It was purely a morality tale, and it actually concluded with bullet points on how to live a better life, with a photo of a genial old man smiling next to his signature.

What follows is exactly what was written on my crisp packet—

" . . . *people from our reunion, in and around our grandparent's 19th century log house. The hot pursuit made its way past some of the ladies of the family and seeing the three original streakers, they started hollering even louder than the boys 'What do you think you're doing?' One lady said.*

After some time and much negotiating (from a safe distance), they promised not to kill me and I gave them their clothes and shoes back. They were still upset and they didn't talk to me for a while.

My **indiscretion** *caused the embarrassment of Bob, my cousins and the ladies of the family. If I'd thought through my decision I may have realised how hurtful it could be.*

Read more about Uncle Ray and for more useful tips on **Discretion**, *visit unclerays.com*

Discretion

'Recognizing and avoiding words, actions and attitudes that could bring undesirable consequences'

Here are simple things to remember to help you demonstrate discretion in every day life.

I Will:

Choose my words carefully

Practice good manners

Listen to criticism

Not make fun of others

Turn down an invitation to do wrong

For more info visit characterfirst.com From my family to yours, thank you for choosing Uncle Ray's"

Now I can't fault the sentiment, but I hope that the majority of Americans don't require their 'chips' to give them moral guidance on a daily basis.

(When I got back to the UK, and after a lot of emailing back and forth between Uncle Rays and me, we concluded that the import tax for small purchases (I could only afford to buy one box) made the chances of me getting any crispy moral guidance in the UK very slim.)

So there I lay; naked on my bed, one leg in the air. At my side, a packet of religious crisps rapidly staining my fingertips red with dubious chilli powder and my mind with even more dubious instructions for life. In my free hand, a can of high strength lager covered in occult-like symbols, as I watched the horror channel on TV with the curtains drawn in the middle of the afternoon. The clothes I had been wearing constantly for the last few days slowly filled the room with a cloud of steam that threatened to strip the seventies wallpaper from the walls. I had twenty-four hours to get well enough to ride and no dry clothes to leave the room in.

I'm assuming that the Mark Twain museum and the surrounding town of Hannibal are all things 'Huckleberry,' but

Finns hadn't turned out the way I'd planned, and unfortunately, I wasn't going to be able to say I'd Sawyer this Tom to the place.

[Homage to *Lost in Translation*]

(I'm not apologising for that.)

I spoke to the family on the phone, and everyone was concerned about my leg, but I thought I'd better tell them, in case it got worse.

Hoping for another quick, early start tomorrow. I've got to go further tomorrow, now I'm not stopping in St. Louis and I'm not sure how this will affect my leg. Probably not good. Ho hum. At least the weather is due to be better tomorrow.

I slept fitfully on and off through the afternoon and night wondering what lay ahead of me.

[This seriously felt like a 1950s themed motel]

Thursday 9th July 2015

HANNIBAL
("AMERICA'S HOMETOWN")

MEMPHIS (TN)
("THE VOLUNTEER STATE")
(. . . THEY LITERALLY NICKNAME EVERYTHING!)

*Well, turns out I didn't need to get to Memphis until the 10th—
I'm a day early(!), and I didn't need to drive four hundred miles
in one day through pouring rain and steaming sunshine . . . but
it's what I did anyway. I am a fool. Luckily, Jared and Ashley are
lovely young people and happy to let me sleep on their lounge floor
for a night, instead of making me find somewhere else in town (they
have other guests tonight, so no room in the inn).*

The journey started well back in Hannibal; it was dry (as were my
clothes finally). My leg felt better than the day before, and although
still painful, my options were slim. I checked out without seeing
Charles and loaded up the bike that nobody had seen fit to steal in
the night. Filled the tank at the alcoholic's favourite filling station
next door and hit the highway to follow plans that I'd cunningly
formulated the night before while listening to American children
not drowning outside my room.

This was going to be easy. St. Louis might be a little hairy trying
to skirt around the outside, as it often is trying to avoid major cities,
but either side looked simple enough—straight down the famous
Highway 61, bit of hassle around the edges of St. Louis, and then

a straight drive down Interstate 55 to Memphis. South all the way and three states in one day—Missouri, Arkansas, and ending in Tennessee. Not a bad plan.

Highway 61 Revisited was released on 30th August 1965, Bob Dylan's sixth studio album, and the first track on the album is 'Like a Rolling Stone.'

I revisited Highway 61 that morning, and it pissed on me.

Again.

At this rate, I would be gathering a considerable amount of moss.

The weather was not as bad as the day before, but I was still soaked through to the skin. Luckily, I dried in the sunshine that followed.

I even ate some cooked food. Stopping for fuel every hundred or so miles, I eventually pulled into a Burger King that was lurking nearby and had breakfast at student o'clock (11AM); a Whopper meal with a coffee, and for lunch I became a patron of McDonalds by purchasing something called an 'iced frappe' (large), which was effectively an ice cold coffee.

I was pleased at the McDonalds when a guy cutting the grass outside came over to me as I was getting back on the bike to say one word—'Nice' (which was nice). Actually, some other guy in a car said something to me about the bike as I walked into the Burger King earlier that morning, but I didn't catch it, so I just smiled, and he seemed happy enough with that. Later, when getting some fuel further down south, a black girl behind the counter started flirting with me, asking if she could have my glasses and how as soon as I spoke she had recognised my accent.

'Oh, you're British. I'm thinking . . . Welsh?'

'No, Cornish.'

'Oh, that's nearby,' her accent slow and syrup laden, she turns to her girlfriends to explain, 'that's southern British,' and they giggle.

The bike was attracting attention, which was all positive, but reminded me about the warnings I had heard about it getting nicked and so always parked where I could keep an eye on it.

Now the rain was a thing of the past, I headed down the Mississippi, and every mile seemed to get hotter as I rode. By the time I got to the McDonalds, I was looking for shade and something to replace my sweating. I'd love to have taken off my heavy leather and helmet to ride, but the former was a necessity, due to the insane American drivers, and the latter, a legal requirement now I was heading down towards the Mason-Dixon Line.

Actually, there are only three states that don't enforce a helmet law for bikers (Illinois, Iowa, and New Hampshire), and I had already ridden in two of them on this trip. As I entered the Confederate states, I felt the protection out-weighed the hassle of a sweaty head.

Being undertaken is a novel experience. Being undertaken and overtaken at the same time at seventy miles an hour on a motorbike, less so in America. They don't give a shit. Indicators are for pussies, and the idea that it's any of your business which lane I might choose to place myself at high speed is the talk of commie bedwetting types. But, and here's the thing; it starts to get under your skin after a while, until eventually you find yourself having a go. I don't recommend this behaviour, of course, but it is quite exhilarating to undertake an articulated lorry at speed, not knowing if he'll suddenly pull across your bike and crush you to a grisly death as he cracks open another cold can of soda and hums along to some Hank Williams on the radio. But the excitement of popping out of that particular cold, shady tunnel back into the hot sunshine of the empty highway is quite addictive. I only did it a couple of times when I absolutely had to, and I chose to speed up to ninety to reduce the truck driver's opportunity. It's a stupid law, and I repeat: I do not recommend you avail yourself of the opportunity when it presents itself to you. We have some of the safest drivers in the UK, and although you may find that hard to accept through your personal experiences on our roads, it becomes very clear when you visit the rest of the world. If our ratio is one in ten morons, the rest of the world isn't happy until at least fifty per cent of all vehicles are piloted by space cadets.

Riding around on the Indian has given me a few near heart attacks, and yet I've grown fond of the behemoth.

The bike hasn't given me any problems when running and has been fine everywhere I've taken it. I'm beginning to like it a bit. I've started calling it 'Babe.' I'm not sure why. The engine is huge; it's like a racing car when it starts up—I've gotta record the sound before I give it back!

And so I continued down the Interstates for most of the day (the best part of four hundred miles and seven hours, all in), the sunshine boiling my brain and the traffic building up and ebbing away, depending on how close to a city we became.

Memphis trivia fans—The city is named after the ancient capital of Egypt on the river Nile and guess what? The first thing you see as you ride into the city is a massive glass/steel pyramid on the outskirts. It's a bloody weird thing to see when you're not expecting it. It was originally some sort of sports arena, then empty for eleven years, and now it's a retail outlet and bowling alley (obviously). Pharaoh-nuff, I say.

But by the time I finally drove over the Hernando de Soto Bridge into Memphis I was pooped. As soon as I could find a spot to pull in, I checked the dwindling battery on my phone and called my AIRBNB hosts for tonight, hoping to get some directions to find their house in the city.

It was whilst talking to the lady of the house, Ashley, and wiping beads of sweat from my eyebrows in what felt like 40 degree heat that I discovered I was a day early, and I wasn't meant to be in Memphis until tomorrow. They were fully booked up. No room at the inn.

Double bugger.

I sounded desperate enough, and so she put me onto her husband, Jared, who offered me the floor of their lounge for the night (at no cost), which I obviously accepted on the proviso that they let me pay them something. With Jared sending me directions, and after a few wrong turns, I ended up outside a terrace of new houses and finally parked the bike. Ashley and Jared came out to meet me, and I heard her say to her husband, 'He looks hot!' Which I thought was a bit racey.

It was only later I realised she was actually commenting on my sweaty head.

They were Christians, and this was their first, and quite small, house, so I had to engage sociable Alex for the first time on this journey at a point when all I wanted to do was cool down and go to sleep. But engage we did, and they were good enough to be extremely accommodating to this weary traveller, feeding me ice cold water and giving up what little privacy they had. They had a three bedroom house, of which two bedrooms were AIRBNB-ed out to two nurses and an unconnected bloke, who would all be leaving tomorrow, when I would take one of the rooms for a couple of days. Ashley and Jared were expecting their first baby in about a month and were a lovely, if somewhat intense, couple. Jared was a teacher, so we chatted about our experiences and bonded over craft beer.

It felt like I'd landed on my feet a bit with these two, and they made it really easy to relax after the longest day on the bike. They brought a mattress down for me to lie on and left me to it by eleven o'clock. It didn't take me long to drift off.

[Not affected by the journey at all]

Friday 10th July 2015

MEMPHIS (TN)
("HOME OF THE BLUES")

Woke up a few times in the night but eventually rose around 6.30 to change my clothes before anyone came downstairs. I'm gonna venture out into Memphis on foot this morning and try and see Beale Street and Sun Studios (the latter being quite nearby theoretically). The temperature is set to soar to the mid-thirties later, which sounds fun.

And that's exactly what I did. I walked to Sun Studios and did the first tour of the day, which was really interesting and well delivered with good humour and detail. The artefacts were amazing: Sam Phillips mobile tape recorder, Ike Turner's guitar and the actual broken amp used to record 'Rocket 66' (the first rock'n'roll record), clothes from Elvis and Johnny Cash. And then we went down into the recording studio itself, still in use in the evenings, where the legendary recordings took place.

Elvis paid four dollars to record his first song in here and I paid twelve to have a look around and stand on the cross taped to the floor where he once sang.

I took some photos and tried to soak up the atmosphere. It wasn't hard to do. The place oozed history. Part museum, part working studio, Sun is a very special place for anyone interested in music. I stood still in the waiting room where Elvis first entered the building and silently breathed in the air, trying to will time to rerun that moment before me.

[Outside Sun Studios]

[Inside Sun Studios, artefacts from the birth of Rock'n'Roll. This truly felt like a 'holy' place, if there is such a thing.]

[The legendary Sun Studio]

The sun was shining outside as I stepped out onto the sidewalk, and the first thing I saw was an old 1950s Cadillac parked in front of the building. I went over to the old gentleman that clearly owned it and complimented him. He gave me his card. It read, 'Tad Pierson— fellow traveller.' He rented out his car and services as a driver to give people tours of Memphis and was, unsurprisingly, fully booked that day, so I was out of luck. After taking a couple of shots of the old car, I wandered across the intersection to one end of Beale Street.

It was the wrong end of Beale Street.

This end of the famous music centre of Memphis was the industrial arse-end of nowhere. But it was Beale Street, so like Muddy Waters before me, I started walking. In the mid-morning sun. Alone.

It was only after I'd been walking for twenty minutes that I realised how vulnerable I was: A white bloke on his own, clearly not where he should be walking, and no witnesses to what might occur. I tried to think positive thoughts as I passed empty car lots and the rear service areas of bigger buildings on either side. There weren't many cars around, and the only people I saw were heading away from where I was going. All were old, black, and clearly poor. I tried to look poor. It seemed to work, because after nearly an hour, in the boiling sunshine, singing 'Mad Dogs and Englishmen' to myself and sweating like a sweaty thing, I ended up at the outskirts of civilization un-mugged and in dire need of something cold and liquid-like in a glass.

Obviously, I went into the first bar I came to: The Tin Roof.

The bar was completely empty, apart from four very pneumatic young ladies desperate to take my order. We got all the way through the ordering process when they suddenly asked for ID. I pointed to my grey beard and asked if they were joking. But they weren't. They said it was Tennessee law that no-one was allowed to sell alcohol without checking all IDs.

I couldn't believe it. I was a bloody long walk away from my ID and completely sweaty.

Agggghhhh!

I staggered back out onto the sidewalk, stood in the shadows, and tried to think what to do next. Then I noticed a sign for something called the Rock'n'Soul Museum, so I thought I'd go in there, where they had to have air conditioning, and cool down for a bit. Another twelve dollars and I was ushered into a lovely cold room to watch a patchy documentary about the history of music in Memphis. After that, we were handed headphones and expected to tour the exhibits in our own time, listening to stuff as we went. My sweaty head couldn't be doing with headphones, and so I left them off and wandered around on my own. The exhibits were okay—some original stuff like more Elvis clothes and another recording desk from Sun Studios (another one?), Ike Turner's knackered old piano, a motorbike used on the cover of a soul album, etc., but mostly a lot of enlarged photographs. For people with no knowledge, it would've been a good place to learn, but for me it was a little boring, and as I'd cooled down now, I slipped through and back outside quite quickly. Apparently, its connected to the Smithsonian Institute in some way, which explains a lot. I'd just been to Sun Studios, and this wasn't a patch on that experience.

By now, I was resigned to walking back to Jared and Ashley's, so I did, cursing myself (and the stupid Tennessee law makers) all the way. It was slightly shorter than my earlier trudge, and I grabbed my driver's licence and headed straight back the way I'd come. I WAS going to have a cold beer, or die trying.

By the time I got back to Beale Street, I'd decided that I wouldn't be going back to The Tin Roof bar to get my thirst quenched, regardless. Directly across the road was the dive bar that I'd chosen to glare at The Tin Roof from as I drank my beer and handed them all the money that The Tin Roof could've had, if they hadn't been such a bunch of arseholes.

[Walking to Memphis–across the flyover and down to Beale Street]

This new place was called Handy's (which was handy), or to give it it's full name, 'Club Handy.' WC Handy was a famous blues guitarist around the time BB King started. I assume the bar was named after him and not as a homage to a scouse *Big Brother* contestant from the UK with some DIY skills.

Now bear in mind what you've just read, and imagine how I reacted when I ordered my first ice cold bottle of cider at the bar and they didn't ask to see my ID.

They didn't ask, to see, my ID.

After a couple of drinks, I asked why not, and the barmaid said she could see I was over twenty-one.

I felt justified in my hatred of the Tin Roof tin heads.

The other major advantage Handy's had over all other bars was that they rolled up an entire wall of the building and suddenly we were allowed to smoke inside. I don't know what rule or regulation they had just sidestepped, but I liked their style. It was only a shame that I had given up smoking six months previously. It was here that I discovered Angry Orchard Hard Cider. The cider that tasted of Granny Smith's apples. I bought two bottles at a time to make up a pint and had soon emptied their supply entirely, thus becoming a local.

Other things about Handy's that I noticed included that they had brown toilet paper in the men's bogs (just think about that for a second), they clearly didn't have a two beer maximum when it came to Cornishmen, as some people visiting the States have claimed (it probably says more about them than it does about America), and that there was an incredible, white pimp-mobile parked permanently across the street that people kept having their photos taken beside.

[Jerry Lee Lewis's Pimp-Mobile on a Beale (side) Street]

They also had the largest standing fan that I'd ever seen and were happy to let me park a table in front of it to dry my sweaty body as I drank their cider supply.

> *Eventually, the place started to come to life, and a blues band put on a show in a little square beside the bar. The bass player was about to go on tour with the 'Janice' band (a band from a forthcoming film about Janice Joplin). He looked a little like Micky Rourke, to be honest, but was nice to chat to. He claimed to be seventy years old, but looked fifty.*
>
> *By the middle of the afternoon, I was feeling peckish, and on recommendation of the barmaid, crossed the street to Dyers for one of their legendary burgers.*

This is what their own website (at dyersonbeale.com) has to say—

> 'Back in 1912, the late Elmer "Doc" Dyer opened his own cafe and began to develop a secret cooking process for the uniquely delicious world famous burgers we still serve here today on Beale Street. Legend has it that the "secret" was Doc Dyer's ageless cooking grease. This famous grease, strained daily, has continued to produce our juicy Dyer's Burgers for over a century now. One of "Doc's" original employees, Mr. Kahn Aaron bought the establishment in 1935 and continued the Dyer's name and tradition of famous burgers. The Dyer's legacy continues to this day.
>
> Over the years, this famous cooking grease has been transported to our various Memphis locations under the watchful protection of armed police escorts, finally settling here on Historic Beale Street, Home of the Blues and World Famous Dyer's!'

Voted the third best burger in America by *Playboy* magazine and the forty-third (out of sixty) things worth shortening your life for by *Esquire* magazine.

I walked in and ordered a basic burger, because at this stage I only had a barmaid's word for what a good burger joint this place was. Boy, was I steered in the right direction. Dyer's burger was the best I had ever tasted. It felt like a coronary wrapped in oil, but it tasted like nectar from an angel's arse. Oh my. I have now found my death row final meal option—I'll have ten Dyer's burgers and a large Coke please; if that doesn't kill me, then you can zap what's left.

The seat I was sitting on wasn't attached to its base, and the service was slow, but the food easily made up for that. If Memphis was ever raised to the ground and this place was the only thing standing, I'd still go back there in a (final) heartbeat just to taste another Dyer's burger.

After my burger, I headed straight back to the bar to continue drinking them dry of Angry Orchard. Finished them and had to start on something called Red Rock, which was also cider but not as nice. Had a few of them, and by now I'd migrated to sitting at the bar and got into a conversation with a bloke who was an electrician. We chatted for a while about this and that, and I learnt all about the state laws on handguns (it seems to be an important topic for men around these parts) and how you were allowed to have one on display in your car and where you couldn't show one off. It seemed to me that the desire to wave a hand gun around people was important to the fellow, so I kept my weak liberal views to myself and agreed with him at every turn, just in case he felt the urge to whip out his rod and pump me full of something unpleasant.

I think my total of bottled ciders had got into the mid-teens when I decided to walk back to Jared's.

By now I was drunk, and I got back by shear will power and sweat. Luckily, when I arrived, nobody was home and so, remembering Ashley's offer of a clothes wash, I bundled my sweaty things on the table, left a note, and went to bed. I was so tired.

I still woke up a few times in the night wondering where Julie and the kids were and falling back into a restless slumber.

Saturday 11th July 2015

MEMPHIS (TN)
('BLUFF CITY'/'BITHPLACE OF ROCK'N'ROLL' . . .
& BEST OF ALL, 'BARBECUED PORK CAPITAL OF THE WORLD')

Tonight is my last night in Memphis, (J&A are fully booked),
so I'll have to move on. I fully intend to see Graceland today, and I
think I'll take the bike as it's a bit too far to walk. They spoke about
the traffic build up yesterday at Sun Studios, so I'm a bit dubious,
but we'll see.

Well, I thought about it for a while and then realised I'd have
to carry my helmet around with me (and my heavy biker jacket). In
these temperatures (late thirties), I thought perhaps not and ordered
a taxi instead. Thirty-five dollars seemed a bit steep, but the journey
did take a while, and I'd never have found it on my own in that time,
on the bike, so I guess it wasn't too bad. When I got there I joined the
throng and queued up for twenty minutes. I opted for the cheapest
tour, which was just the house and gardens, because of the massive
mark-up to have a gawp at his cars and planes. It went from thirty-five
for my ticket to seventy for the full automotive experience.

The ticket sold to me at 11AM was for the midday shuttle, but
as they do eight shuttles an hour and I was on number seven, my
actual journey wasn't due to start for an hour and forty. So, time
to kill in the Elvis complex, which housed the ticket shop across
the road from our actual destination. This complex contained
something like nine different Elvis memorabilia shops, a few Elvis
themed restaurants, and the car museum. I had a catfish sandwich,
which tasted better than it sounds, and avoided buying any over-

priced tourist tat. It was steaming outside, so loitering within the shops became a necessity, just to have the air conditioning. The queue for the shuttle was outside though, and I was sweating like a dog when I finally got on board the bus that took us over the road to the front door of Graceland.

[Graceland–the home of the King of Rock'n'Roll]

There was a little chat from the tour guide telling me nothing I didn't already know about Graceland or Elvis, and then we were instructed to put on our headphones and listen to a guided tour that someone had recorded.

Inside the house it was cramped with all the people, but I soon stepped it up by not using the iPad and headphones and merely zipping through with my iPhone, snapping photos as I went. The virtual guided tour is a practicality, I understand, but it leaves me cold. Give me a human (like at Sun Studios) anytime.

Being inside his home was a strange experience and not what I'd imagined. I thought it would be an interesting thing to do, but it became quite an emotional thing. I'm not religious and have never had that reverence, but here within the walls where he actually walked, the door frames his hands must've touched, I did feel something close to a religious experience. I found myself holding my breath and trying to be alone at points. When the headphone wearing crowds had passed on, I loitered, and it did feel like ghosts were passing around me. It was cold inside, but there didn't appear to be any air conditioning. The basement bar and pool room felt very personal, and I imagined Elvis hiding down here, below ground, while the press snapped photos from the road a few hundred yards away. Privacy in a public life. And yet the house wasn't hidden from the road and was ostentatious in its day—a sign that the local poor boy had actually made it. The wealthy these days prefer to hide away behind high walls and acres of land, but back then this so-called mansion was a symbol of local success.

[It's smaller than you'd have expected, but you can understand why they had to move . . .]

[The back garden at Graceland. No swing-ball. Strange.]

Seriously though, it's a tiny house. I think I've lived in bigger houses myself, and I've never lived in something claiming to be a mansion. But it is what it is (whatever that means), and it's where the king of rock'n'roll lived and died. In fact, the toilet on which he actually died is directly above the unsuspecting visitors as they enter the house, although the upstairs is strictly out of bounds to everyone except the surviving Presleys. As far as I'm aware, only three people have been upstairs in Graceland since he died; Priscilla, Lisa Marie, and on one time only, against all protocol, Nicholas Cage. Even presidents have been refused entry to those private rooms, so I imagine Elvis didn't tidy his bedroom much, either that or they never had the water pressure to flush that final fried peanut butter floater.

The house has been preserved as it was in 1977, so it was nearly fifty years since anyone had actually used that revolutionary (at the time) microwave oven or walked across that Astro Turf (or wondered why he did the ceiling and walls in it too). It's been nearly half a century since anyone put a new battery in that weird clock embedded in that painting that most people walked straight passed without even spotting, and a bloody long time since someone played something from Elvis's minimal record collection (no more than sixty albums on display).

[Our hero captures a painting of Elvis's dad, and a well placed knob]

In his back garden he had a separate cinema (as you do), a building that originally housed a squash court (now, wall to wall, floor to ceiling, gold discs), a swimming pool (not shaped like a guitar, surprisingly), and a paddock for some horses. So in fact, it turns out that the humble front of Graceland does actually hide quite a spread of private land behind.

It was a time capsule from nearly fifty years ago and felt both genuine and unreal at the same time. The grave was nice though—a fitting end to a tour after the gaudiness of all the trophies and stage wear. A beautiful house, but smaller than you'd imagine.

[He had a couple of hit records, that Elvis chap]

I caught a shuttle back to the other side of the road and then a taxi back to Beale Street for a cider at Handy's to gather my thoughts after an extraordinary afternoon. I hadn't expected the emotional connection that I felt as I walked around Elvis Presley's home, not being an Elvis fanatic, as most people around me seemed to be. But I have never been anywhere like that in my life before, and the couple of hours that I took to mooch around (you're not on any kind of schedule to move along—take as long as you like) have stayed with me years later. I've been to the Beatles' homes in Liverpool and the place John was shot in New York City, I've been to the recreation of the Cavern Club and to Sun Studios, to Abbey Road and Birdland, but nowhere has left its mark on me like Graceland did. Perhaps you have to like Elvis a bit and have an open mind, but I'd advise anyone with an interest in popular music to visit if they get a chance. Perhaps it's our Mecca, or something, but Memphis stays with you when you leave.

As the bar filled up, I wandered next door to the building that had that pimp-mobile parked outside, which turned out to be Jerry Lee Lewis's bar (and his old car), to see a live rock'n'roll band (and a six year old singer—don't ask!). The barman bought me a drink, when I told him I had no more money, which was bloody nice of him, but eventually, I had to take the inevitable long walk home. The sun always shining and everyone else with a sense of purpose that I couldn't connect with.

[The final resting place. I was in Newlyn catching shrimps from rock pools when it happened, so you can't blame me!]

Back at Ashley's and Jared's, I paid for us all to have a takeaway pizza for our last meal together and to say thank you for being so hospitable. Jared drove me to 'Little Italy' on Union Avenue, where we picked up a large pizza, a stromboli, and some garlic bread, before popping next door to a supermarket for some craft beers. The only stromboli I'd ever heard of was something to do with Pinocchio, so I had to see what this thing was. There were no strings involved:

It turned out to be a sort of rolled pizza, Swiss roll type thing. Nice, but very filling. It was an expensive meal (and way too much for me to finish) but worth it to show how much I appreciated this young, open minded couple.

After a long evening/night talking and laughing over the food and beer, I bid my new friends goodnight and farewell, as I'd be leaving early in the morning to avoid the traffic and heat, and went upstairs to my bed.

Sunday 12th July 2015

MEMPHIS (TN)

TEXARKANA (TX)
("THE LONE STAR STATE")

I loaded up the bike and noticed that the footrest had sunk into the melted tarmac. So it had been quite hot then, it wasn't just me.

Out on the road once more, I headed southwest, away from the Mississippi for the first time on my journey.

Something had changed. I intended to ride down to New Orleans then race over to Irving in Dallas to drop the bike off and fly home, but over the days in Memphis, I'd realised a few things. Firstly, the $30,000 motorbike was ridiculously ostentatious, and I was taking it into a part of the country that was fundamentally poor, armed, and historically, some might say, within its rights to kick the living shit out of a white man. It also became financially disturbing when I found out that I was liable for $1,000 if the bike was stolen. The lure of the South had waned in me, and now I had to figure out what I wanted to do with the remaining days.

Soon, I was on my way towards Little Rock. I thought I might just jack the whole journey in and return home early, now that I'd decided not to go to New Orleans. I'd spoken to Julie about it, and she understood. I still wasn't sure what I was going to do. The journey was easy along Interstate 40 and then 30 into Texarkana, where I finally stopped at a Holiday Inn at midday. The best part *of $100 for one night made it an expensive place to stay, but I was closer to where I had to drop the bike off.*

I think if I didn't have the Indian, I would've kept to my original plan, but I'd lost faith in the journey. My usual solo travelling style offers no opportunity for confrontation (I look like I've got nothing worth nicking and I don't look like a tourist), whereas this time I was waving a wad of cash at everyone who saw me, screaming, 'Rob me! Rob me! I'm clearly not from around these parts!'

I wasn't going to see America from the inside anymore while on this bike, and it was too late to change it for something less obvious. If I left the bike somewhere and went on foot, it'd get nicked and I'd lose $1,000, and if it didn't, I'd be worried that it would, which would ruin what time I had left anyway.

I was also injured. My leg was still painful and kept reminding me about the outcome of blood clots—if they stay in one place, the pressure builds up behind them, rupturing the veins, if they move, there's a chance they might stick in your heart and cause a heart attack. Add that to sitting on an aircraft at 30,000 feet, and you may get an idea where my head was at.

So I did what I could; tried to empty my mind and just enjoy the ride.

Along the Interstates, it was smooth and sunny but not as hot as it had been. The traffic was busier as I chose roads leading towards Dallas, but like anywhere, when the roads lead towards cities, the traffic builds. I was glad to stop off at Texarkana.

I was given a disabled room for some reason, but it had much more space, so I wasn't complaining, and I relaxed for the afternoon and evening after a shower, checking emails, and lounging around.

At one point, I opened the curtain to the only window in the room and saw my view—a waterpark slide. Lovely. Now I'll get accused of being a pervert if I sit and watch those kids going down the slide. I pulled the thing shut again and lay down, like a starfish, on the massive bed and drifted off to sleep

Monday 13th July 2015

TEXARKANA (TX)
("THE TEXAS SLIDE")

DALLAS (TX)
("BIG D")

Another rough night, trying to decide what to do, but by the morning my mind was set on a decision. I was going to try and drop the bike early, go to the airport, and beg to get on an earlier flight home. The journey was done. My mistakes had caught up with me, and the dream was over.

I felt relieved to have finally made the choice and had a sense of direction once more.

Setting out on Interstate 30, heading into the morning sun as soon as I could. I left behind half a bottle of Jim Beam, my off-bike jeans in the bin, and the usual shrapnel of change. I was filled with the desire to get home and left without breakfast.

> *My destination was Irving in Dallas—a wing and a prayer for my iPhone's dodgy sat nav to get me to my end point, where I'd be able to drop off the bike and get a taxi to the airport. What happened there would be in the lap of the gods, but theoretically, I could be back in the UK by the end of tomorrow (due to the loss of hours on the return flight). It was six hours behind in Dallas, but my official flight was five days ahead.*

209

The heat started to rise as I ran the road on the Indian for our last day together. I stopped for cold drinks and fuel, finally pulling into one of those 'truck stops' that occur where you can use the toilet and buy shit from machines. They are never manned stations, just a pull-in for the essentials. Also, bizarrely, they aren't always on the right side of the road (beside the slow lane); sometimes they sit between the traffic on what we might call the central reservation (although they probably wouldn't, for obvious reasons). So you find yourself coming off the road from the fast lane doing seventy into a car park full of stationary cars. It's a bit hairy, I can tell you, when you're hoping for a quick slash and a can of Coke, hitting a parking lot at that speed.

As always, the car park was full of trucks and pickups. I rarely, if ever, saw another bike at these stops. Even at the fuel stops they seemed to hunt in pairs or trios and used the other filling station option across the road from me. I got the odd wave from other solo bikers, but they never spoke to me. The rarity of bikes on the roads here made me wonder at the lack of empathy to fellow riders, but you can't judge the majority by the few I came across, I guess.

As I got back to the bike after getting my cold can, an old fellow was standing by it with a young daughter/granddaughter. As seems quite normal out here, he had a long white moustache and was built with an extra belly. He was as tall as me, and I reckon, in his seventies. I felt no fear; his demeanour was of someone in an art gallery studying an old master, and when I arrived, he complimented me on the bike, saying it was 'pretty' (but not in a bad way). He introduced his granddaughter (probably around 12/13 years old), and we talked about bikes and how he'd love to still ride, but his wife wouldn't let him anymore because he was too old.

An ex-military man, I could see the dreams in his eyes and felt sorry for him. Then his wife joined us, and he was quietly dragged off to his SUV, the shackles back on once more.

The encounter raised my spirits. I could've done with a few more of those in the last few days, but most people seemed to avoid me when I stopped. Perhaps bikers had a worse reputation than I imagined out here.

I was used to the bike by now and sat confidently on her as we pulled out of the stop point and into traffic with ease. It felt right to be on the bike, hammering along the concrete with the sun beating down on my black helmet and armoured leathers. I was now able to spot (and acknowledge in time) other bikers as they passed, heading in the other direction. Only twice in the whole journey did bikes pass me in the same direction, and both gave me a reassuring wave of a fellow biker. The most impressive being from a guy on a chop wearing colours. That made me feel less alone in amongst all the trucks and speeding pickups.

But now I was heading into that horrendous metropolis, Dallas, like a twig caught in a whirlpool. The first major American city I had ridden into (Memphis doesn't really feel like a city), and unlike St. Louis, this was one journey I couldn't avoid.

It didn't take long to notice the build-up of traffic as we headed towards the city. The gaps between the lorry trains became smaller and less frequent. The speed of the traffic seemed to be faster, although it probably wasn't, just more in number starting to take up road space. The exits came more often, and all manner of fast moving vehicles shot onto Interstate 30 to join us. At one point, a car joined us on the right from a feeder lane and, without indicating once, literally just went diagonally across three lanes of traffic in front of me to the fast lane. I did what any sane person would do and nearly shit myself.

Everyone seemed to know where they were going except me, but I stuck to my guns and only occasionally undertook when I was convinced the trucks weren't going to kill me (I was never convinced).

Soon I was moving from a three lane highway to a four, five, and finally, six lane insanity loop. Lanes kept joining us, and with them, whole loads more traffic, all slopping across traffic (mostly without indicators), like they had never seen any car crashes in the movies. Unfortunately, I had.

This part of the journey quickly became the most stressful of the whole trip, as I had to watch literally left, right, in front, and behind, all at the same time. These bastards were insane. Trying to keep an eye on the fuel gauge and remember what road number I was meant to be on was driving me nuts, plus we kept speeding up and then coming to a stop and then crawling along at five miles an hour in the steaming mid-day sun. As anyone who's ever ridden a bike will tell you, slow speeds are far harder to ride than faster ones.

Not only balancing becomes an issue, but also clutch control makes
your hand ache. Add to that the other road users, and even Brian
Wilson would be struggling to have 'Fun, fun, fun.'

I pulled off the Interstate with a third of a tank of fuel left and
more than a hundred and fifty miles to go (theoretically) to my
final destination on East Irving Boulevard, somewhere in North
Dallas. Fuel was required. That, and a chance to double check what
roads I was aiming to be on once in the city. I mean, technically,
the Interstate circumnavigates the city, but I have to know when to
jump off to hit Irving, or like the M25 around London, I might be
burning up valuable petrol going around in circles.

When I say 'valuable,' it's not expensive or anything, it's just the
hassle of finding another filing station to top the bike up. I mean,
fuel is dirt cheap in America, but I didn't fancy crawling around the
outskirts of Dallas for any more hours than I had to, just waiting for
that high speed pickup to ram me off the road.

A slurp of cold Coke and a full tank of fuel, and I was back on
the road heading into the mouth of the beast once again. The traffic
built up, and I tried to remember which roads I needed to be on.
Slowly Dallas rose on the skyline before us, and the rollercoaster
started the long drop into the city. All around me were steel death
traps intent on squashing my bike. I stood my ground with the
satisfaction that at least they couldn't see how scared my face was. I
could be anyone on this bike, under all this leather and solid black
helmet, dark visor down. I think a solo biker sends out a message to
other road users that those travelling in twos or three, just don't. It
says, 'I don't need backup; so beware.' (Well, that's what I hoped it
was saying) (either that or, 'They call me, Johnny No Mates.')

> *Slowly the traffic rolled to a crawling speed, practically no faster
> than walking. This was the worst scenario situation for me, because
> of my fear of dropping the bike again. You couldn't keep stopping
> in this type of traffic and then moving on; you had to just go as
> physically slowly as you could without putting a foot down. Also at
> this speed and time of day, the effect of the sun was really started to
> take a hold, and I began to sweat like a pig on a spit.*
>
>   *It lasted for about an hour of tortuous tarmac, before we finally
> rolled faster and faster, and then I was able to pick up the pace.
> Soon, I was back to a steady 50mph and that was the point, in four
> lane traffic, tail to tail, a car shot out from a feeder lane on my*

right into first, then my lane, then lanes three and four, and finally
exiting the Interstate from the fast lane (four) off another feeder
lane. All done at 60mph. All done without an indicator to be seen.
All done right in front of me in such a sweeping move that within
twenty seconds he had vanished and there was no evidence that
anything had happened. No-one slowed down for the idiot; no-
one batted an eyelid. I felt like I was in a bloody death race dream
scene. What next? A bulldozer on the road ahead coming our way
crushing everyone that ploughed into it? As it turned out, that was
the last mental driver that I was going to notice. After that point,
my receptors became less sensitive and I focussed on getting along
the road and finding Irving Boulevard, but my mind wandered . . .

I was skirting over the North of Dallas, just going around the
top of the city with the Interstate traffic, effectively heading out of
the city towards Denton, the home of one of my favourite bands
(Bowling For Soup).

A few years ago, I'd been writing freelance for music papers and
had attempted to get an interview with the band, when I noticed
that they were playing at a festival I was attending. I'd spent a few
feverish days before the event, emailing their press officer and
manager in California, trying to get an okay. (I'd also been trying
to get Blondie, as they were at the same festival, but to no avail.)
I'd used the 'blag it' method quite a lot in an effort to create some
sort of career for myself as a music journalist and had some success
in the review market, but like any megalomaniac, I wanted more.
I wanted features and interviews too. So, anyway, I'd not got a
definite yes or no by the time I'd had to leave for said festival but
had left my mobile number with both camps, not really expecting
much. Day two at the festival; and as I stood in the men's onsite
bathroom with about thirty other blokes draining our bladders and
listening to Motorhead on stage nearby, my mobile phone fired up
in my pocket and startled all of us. 'I bet you can't do that,' I said to
the man on my right as I stood there finishing the job in hand, the
phone still beeping in time to Lemmy's gang.

Outside, it turned out I had an interview with Bowling For
Soup in an hour. Shit.

I'd assumed they'd be no hope and had left my trusty
Dictaphone at home, and my mobile (back in those days) had no
function that could record for longer than a minute or two. The

amount of margarita slush puppies that I'd drunk didn't help me to understand my friend's superior phone apps, so I went with my own tin can and string, hoping to just Nick Kent it. (Nick Kent was a legendary music writer who never recorded his interviews, just remembered them (or made them up afterwards) and wrote what he remembered). With the amount of alcohol I had sliding around my body, I'd be lucky to remember what my own name was, let alone anything the Bowling For Soup boys had to say. To try and look vaguely professional, I pretended my mobile phone was a Dictaphone and placed it face down on the coach seat between lead singer Jaret Reddick and myself and then blagged the interview for half an hour. I can still remember some of it to this day, ten years down the line. It was my first face-to-face interview.

And back to Dallas—I was coming in on Interstate 30, and somewhere in the spaghetti of the city, I had to grab a line on either Interstate 35E or 35W. Much like Rome, Dallas is full of Vespas and sharp dressed Italian men pinching ladies bums and handbags with equal abandon. No. Much like Rome; all roads led towards the city, and circumnavigating it was a mission and a half, but this was not a journey I intended doing twice. The bike had to be returned to an address somewhere in this ant hill, and I was going to find it. I gritted my sweaty teeth and rode along with all the other traffic.

A couple of choices arrived along the way; junctions with names and places, but the wrong Interstate numbers, then junctions with the right numbers but places that I'd never heard of. Effectively, Interstate 35E and the 35W started out south of Dallas as just Interstate 35, then split at the base of the city, formed a balloon shape around the city, and regrouped at the north of Dallas to continue upwards on the map, back to just Interstate 35 again. I had to jump from my original Interstate 30 from Texarkana to Interstate 35E towards Denton, but going through Irving first (where I'd jump off the highway and get down into suburbia and seek out the bike dealers on West Irving Boulevard).

The warren of streets was a nightmare in the heat. Every junction created more opportunities to take the wrong turn and drag this sweaty finale out a little longer. I stopped numerous times to consult the mobile map and ever so slowly inched my way closer to the depot. When it finally came into view, there was a combined sense of relief and disappointment sweeping over me. The journey was over.

[Not looking at the Texas (water) Slide outside his disabled double room, our hero considers what he's learnt by the end of the journey.]

Stage five

Postscript

Looking back on the journey, from New York to Los Angeles and back, and then from Chicago to Dallas on the motorbike, crossing the United States has been an adventure and has, as is often the case, taught me a lot about myself along the way. I've learnt a lot about a country I thought I knew too and about the wide variety of people that live there. I've learnt that it's been a long time since I was really lonely. I've learnt that practically nobody gives a shit about the British accent, that Mexicans are treated like the blacks used to be, and that, as I expected, most people just want to have a good time and chill out.

Hey! But before we go, there's just enough space to fit a final list in—

A List of Some Things I've Learnt From This Journey:
- America does NOT drink weak beer.
- America does love a flag.
- America knows how to run a bloody train service.
- American people are friendly, inquisitive, and generous.
- A lot of Americans really DO believe in God.
- America is probably the most diverse and beautiful country that I've ever seen.
- Americans drive like three-year-olds.
- Americans are welcoming (if you're a white male).

- America is generally quite clean.
- Tennessee does NOT always operate its ID policy.
- Graceland gave me an epiphany.
- Elvis was much less 'Vegas' than you'd imagine.
- Two Americans think I look and sound like Piers Morgan, while a Russian taxi driver thinks I sound Australian.
- LA is a shithole.
- Indian Chiefs are way too heavy (and slightly gay).
- There's a freedom in America that we couldn't live with.
- On the East Coast everyone wears baseball caps.
- On the West Coast nobody walks anywhere.
- Americans consider the Greyhound bus to be only a sidestep up from hitchhiking.
- America is like a family: there's distant cousins, uncles, and aunts who have some strange ideas, there's the ones that married into the family and don't look like everyone else but want to be there because they fell in love, then there's the kids with their rebellious ideas and the mother and father trying to hold it all together. America is a big family; dysfunctional at times, but ultimately tied together, and through thick or thin, good times or bad, America always looks towards the horizon.

I have a lot of faith in the American people. There's more than three hundred million of the buggers spread out across those four time zones, and although the media often portrays them all as a bunch of rednecks and airheads, I can assure you that they are as varied and intelligent as any human beings on the planet could possibly be.

The thing with travelling is that it gives you first-hand examples of life that the media can't edit. It gives you a personal version of the truth that Dave from marketing hasn't had a hand in, and although it can never give you the whole story, it can give you an insight into what the whole story might be. The smells, the tastes, the colours, and the sounds are all things that all forms of media (including literature) can only hint at. To experience life, you have to immerse yourself in it.

So step outside.

Live.

ACKNOWLEDGEMENTS

Thanks to everyone I met along the way that made the journey better and who's names I never got to know; I hope we meet again one day.

Special thanks go to Kara Tabor, Gjoni Bardhyl, Corey Adams, Mike Stax, Bill Cousins, Alan Flora, Neil the Deadhead, Kris Clark, and Jared and Ashly Pitts.

And Janet—I hope you enjoyed the ride x

Also from Road Dog Publications

Those Two Idiots! [1][2] *by A. P. Atkinson*
Mayhem, mirth, and adventure follow two riders across two continents. Setting off for Thailand thinking they were prepared, this story if full of mishaps and triumphs. An honest journey with all the highs and lows, wins and losses, wonderful people and low-lifes, and charms and pitfalls of the countries traveled through.

Motorcycles, Life, and . . . [1][2] *by Brent Allen*
Sit down at a table and talk motorcycles, life and . . . (fill in the blank) with award winning riding instructor and creator of the popular "Howzit Done?" video series, Brent "Capt. Crash" Allen. Here are his thoughts about riding and life and how they combine told in a lighthearted tone.

The Elemental Motorcyclist [1][2] *by Brent Allen*
Brent's second book offers more insights into life and riding and how they go together. This volume, while still told in the author's typical easy-going tone, gets down to more specifics about being a better rider.

A Short Ride in the Jungle [1][2] *by Antonia Bolingbroke-Kent*
A young woman tackles the famed Ho Chi Minh Trail alone on a diminutive pink Honda Cub armed only with her love of Southeast Asia, its people, and her wits.

Mini Escapades around the British Isles [1][2] *by Zoë Cano*
As a wonderful compilation of original short stories closer to home, Zoë Cano captures the very essence of Britain's natural beauty with eclectic travels she's taken over the years exploring England, Ireland, Scotland, and Wales.

Bonneville Go or Bust [1][2] *by Zoë Cano*
A true story with a difference. Zoë had no experience for such a mammoth adventure of a lifetime but goes all out to make her dream come true to travel solo across the lesser known roads of the American continent on a classic motorcycle.

I loved reading this book. She has a way of putting you right into the scene. It was like riding on the back seat and experiencing this adventure along with Zoë. —★★★★ Amazon Review

Southern Escapades[1][2] by Zoë Cano

As an encore to her cross country trip, Zoë rides along the tropical Gulf of México and Atlantic Coast in Florida, through the forgotten backroads of Alabama and Georgia. This adventure uncovers the many hidden gems of lesser known places in these beautiful Southern states.

. . . Zoë has once again interested and entertained me with her American adventures. Her insightful prose is a delight to read and makes me want to visit the same places.—★★★★★ Amazon Review

Chilli, Skulls & Tequila[1][2] by Zoë Cano

Zoe captures the spirit of beautiful Baja California, México, with a solo 3 000 mile adventure encountering a myriad of surprises along the way and unique, out-of-the-way places tucked into Baja's forgotten corners.

Zoe adds hot chilli and spices to her stories, creating a truly mouth-watering reader's feast!—★★★★ Amazon Review

Hellbent for Paradise[1][2] by Zoë Cano

The inspiring—and often nail-biting—tale of Zoë's exploits roaming the jaw-dropping natural wonders of New Zealand on a mission to find her own paradise.

Mini Escapades around the British Isles[1][2] by Zoë Cano

As a wonderful compilation of original short stories closer to home, Zoë Cano captures the very essence of Britain's natural beauty with eclectic travels she's taken over the years exploring England, Ireland, Scotland, and Wales.

Shiny Side Up[1][2] by Ron Davis

A delightful collection of essays and articles from Ron Davis, Associate Editor and columnist for *BMW Owners News*. This book is filled with tales of the road and recounts the joys and foibles of motorcycle ownership and maintenance. Read it and find out why Ron is a favorite of readers of the *Owners News*!

Rubber Side Down[1,2] by Ron Davis
More great stuff from Ron Davis.

[Ron] shares his experiences with modesty and humor, as one who is learning as he goes along. Which is what we all do in real life. And he does what all the best motorcycle writing does: he makes you wonder why you aren't out there riding your own bike, right now...his work simply helps you stay sane until spring." –Peter Egan, Cycle World *Columnist and author of* Leanings 1, 2, and 3, and The Best of Peter Egan.

Beads in the Headlight [1] by Isabel Dyson
A British couple tackle riding from Alaska to Tierra del Fuego two-up on a 31 year-old BMW "airhead." Join them on this epic journey across two continents.

A great blend of travel, motorcycling, determination, and humor. —★★★★★ Amazon Review

Chasing America [1,2] by Tracy Farr
Tracy Farr sets off on multiple legs of a motorcycle ride to the four corners of America in search of the essence of the land and its people.

In Search of Greener Grass [1] by Graham Field
With game show winnings and his KLR 650, Graham sets out solo for Mongolia & beyond. Foreword by Ted Simon

Eureka [1] by Graham Field
Graham sets out on a journey to Kazahkstan only to realize his contrived goal is not making him happy. He has a "Eureka!" moment, turns around, and begins to enjoy the ride as the ride itself becomes the destination.

Different Natures [1] by Graham Field
The story of two early journeys Graham made while living in the US, one north to Alaska and the other south through México. Follow along as Graham tells the stories in his own unique way.

Thoughts on the Road[1,2] by Michael Fitterling
The Editor of *Vintage Japanese Motorcycle Magazine* ponders his experiences with motorcycles and riding and how they've intersected and influenced his life.

Northeast by Northwest [1] [2] *by Michael Fitterling*
The author finds two motorcycle journeys of immense help staving off depression and the other effects of stress. Along the way, he discovers the beauty of North America and the kindness of its people.
. . . one of the most captivating stories I have read in a long time. Truly a MUST read!!—★★★★★ Amazon Review

Hit the Road, Jac! [1] [2] *by Jacqui Furneaux*
At 50, Jacqui leaves her home and family, buys a motorcycle in India, and begins a seven-year world-wide journey with no particular plan. Along the way she comes to terms with herself and her family.

Asphalt & Dirt [1] [2] *by Aaron Heinrich*
A compilation of profiles of both famous figures in the motorcycle industry and relatively unknown people who ride, dispelling the myth of the stereotypical "biker" image.

Chasing Northern Lights [1] [2] *by Miguel Oldenberg*
A Venezuelan immigrant sets out to get to know his new country on the motorcycle ride of a lifetime.

The Tom Report [1] [2] *by Tom Reuter*
Two young men set out from Washinton state on Suzuki DR650 dual sport motorcycles. Join them and a colorful cast of fellow travelers as they wind their way south to the end of the world. Their journey is filled with fun, danger, and even enlightenment.

A Tale of Two Dusters & Other Stories [1] [2] *by Kirk Swanick*
In this collection of tales, Kirk Swanick tells of growing up a gearhead behind both the wheels of muscle cars and the handlebars of motorcycles and describes the joys and trials of riding

Man in the Saddle [1] [2] *by Paul van Hoof*
Aboard a 1975 Moto Guzzi V7, Paul starts out from Alaska for Ushuaia. Along the way there are many twists and turns, some which change his life forever. English translation from the original Dutch.